God's Action in the World

The Bampton Lectures for 1986

Maurice Wiles

XPRESS REPRINTS

1 85931 009 5

First published 1986
by SCM Press Ltd

Reissued 1993 by
XPRESS REPRINTS
SCM Bookroom
26–30 Tottenham Road, London N1 4BZ

Printed in Great Britain by
Antony Rowe Ltd
Chippenham, Wiltshire

CONTENTS

PREFACE

Recent Bampton Lecturers have published their lectures in a much fuller form than it was possible to deliver them. Such a procedure provides scope for a more detailed development of the argument and a fuller discussion of the views of other scholars than is possible in a series of short public lectures, especially ones delivered within the context of an act of worship. Despite those obvious advantages, I have departed from that custom. The lectures are here published almost exactly in the form in which they were delivered. The unusual genre of the 'lecture-sermon' has this to be said for it. It encourages the lecturer to present his argument in a concise form that must seek to carry conviction both intellectually and religiously. These lectures do not aspire to be a comprehensive treatment of the many difficult issues raised by the affirmation of God's action in the world. They are designed rather to encourage a particular way of viewing those issues, which seems to me to be both intellectually and religiously fruitful.

The problems with which they attempt to deal have been a dominant concern in much of my earlier theological writing. What I have tried to do here is to bring out for more direct discussion issues that arise inescapably as an important motif in the treatment of any more specific theological topic. The ideas to which I have tried to give expression are thus the fruit of reflection and discussion over many years. Far more friends, colleagues and pupils have contributed to their formulation during that period than it is possible to mention by name. But some call for special mention. Peter Baelz and Basil Mitchell have both provided a particular stimulus through shared seminars and shared friendship. Gordon Kaufman and Schubert Ogden have been major influences, first through their writings and subsequently through lively but too infrequent occasions of meeting. Specific conversations of a particularly illuminating kind with Christoph Schwöbel and Kathryn Tanner merit grateful recall. David Pailin has added to the help given through many constructive discussions over the years the kindness of reading the manuscript in draft and suggesting ways in which the argument might be improved. None of these, or of the many others with whom I have discussed these issues in the past, bears any responsibility for what I have written – beyond the fact that without the stimulus of their encouragement and help it might never have been written at all.

The SCM Press, in the persons of John Bowden and Linda Foster, have given (not for the first time) much valued help through their personal encouragement and professional expertise. Doreen Abrams, Jane Pusey and Bernadette O'Reilly have shared the typing of various drafts with unfailing cheerfulness and skill. The first of those drafts which have culminated in this book was composed under ideal conditions during a memorable month at the Bellagio Study and Conference Center thanks to the generosity of the Rockefeller Foundation.

MAURICE WILES

I

Where Does God Act?

Does God act in the world? Does he affect what happens to us in the varied experiences of our daily life? If so, in what ways and by what means? Those are the kinds of question which lie behind the line of enquiry I intend to pursue. Wherever they may lead us, there is certainly nothing technical or esoteric about the questions themselves. Time and again in recent years national or international events have drawn them to the attention of the general public, and they have proved to have an irresistible fascination for believer and unbeliever alike. A service of thanksgiving was held in St Paul's to mark the ending of the Falklands War; but there was no agreement about what it was appropriate to thank God for.[1] Part of York Minster was burnt down three days after the consecration of the Bishop of Durham; *The Times* leader-writer (in a leader entitled 'Act of God') found it 'hard not to be reminded of Elijah and the prophets of Baal'.[2] An American airliner was hijacked to Beirut by Shi'ite Muslim gunmen; the pilot, who acted as spokesman for the hostages after their liberation, spoke of how the Lord had taken very good care of them.[3] The form in which this question of God's action was brought into the public forum on each of those occasions was a source of profound embarrassment to many a reflective Christian. The moral implications of the implicit or explicit claims involved in each case were devastating. Does God take the British side in war? Does he, like Zeus, send out thunderbolts in his displeasure? Where was his care for the hostages when one of them was murdered and his corpse thrown out on to the tarmac?

It is easy to find fault with such naive accounts of what are said to be examples of God's action. But when so many of the particular cases in which communities or individuals find themselves led to speak of God's acting prove to be cases which appear to others both morally and spiritually unacceptable, we need to give thought to the deeper underlying issue. Writing to *The Guardian*, the Archbishop of York, John Habgood, declared that where he 'would want to part company with those who interpret the recent fire in York Minster as evidence of divine wrath is not on the question whether God can or cannot intervene, but on the character of God as revealed by the events which some wish to ascribe directly to Him'.[4] We may applaud the Archbishop's chosen emphasis on the moral issue of the character of God implicit in the suggestion that the fire at York Minster was an act of divine retribution for the consecration of the Bishop of Durham. But was he right to dismiss the more general issue concerning the possibility of divine intervention as such, as one on which Christian agreement could be readily assumed? Ought we to take it for granted that every Christian is bound to give an unqualifiedly positive response to my initial question – Does God act in the world?

No question is more fundamental to Christian theology today. Admittedly it assumes a positive answer to the prior question of God's existence. But if we were to affirm the existence of God without being able to go on and say something about his activity in relation to the world, we would have done little of significance for religious faith. It is what God does as creator and redeemer that has always been seen as crucial both for Christian faith and for Christian theology. Walter Kasper speaks for many others when he says: 'The God who no longer plays an active role in the world is in the final analysis a dead God.'[5] Deism is widely regarded as no different from atheism, as far as religious practice or religious viability is concerned.

Yet the notion of God's acting in the world is highly problematical. Nor are the difficulties inherent in the notion simply the invention of modern scepticism. Even if it is true that they are felt in a particularly acute way at the present time, they are not wholly new. The notion has been problematic throughout Christian history, and it is important to recall that fact as we embark on our search for an appropriate understanding of it in our own day. Admittedly, what makes it problematic is not something that has remained unchanged through the centuries. There is a difference between the ways in which the difficulty is most often felt today and the ways in which it was mainly experienced in the early formative centuries of Christian thought. And that difference is not merely a matter of degree; it concerns where the heart of the problem lies. Some brief consideration of the nature of that difference offers, therefore, a useful way in to the study of our central theme. The contrast can be set out in very general terms in this way. One important conviction within the Hellenistic world in which early Christianity developed was the utter changelessness of God. The tradition that springs particularly from the Plato of the *Phaedo* stresses the radical separation of the divine from the phenomenal realm of our experience. The essential nature of the divine was precisely its freedom from the transience of the phenomenal world. Would it not then be a contradiction in terms to speak of God as an agent involved in the changing scene of that passing world of human experience? Yet clearly that is what Judaeo-Christian faith had to do, if it was not to abandon its traditions altogether. For at the heart of that faith was the idea of God's intimate involvement with the history of a people. The fundamental source of the distinctive Jewish belief in God was the experience reflected in the story of the Exodus and the Jews' recognition of themselves as a particular people with a particular history and a particular destiny; in other words their faith in God was grounded in the discovery of a profound meaning within the particular events of history. For the first Christians this understanding of God was reinforced by their conviction that he had acted decisively in Jesus and was very much at work in the emergence and establishment of the Christian church. They knew that God was at work in the world; they knew where

God was at work in the world. That was not in doubt; that was not where for them the problem lay. Their problem was how these unquestioned data of faith could be true of a God whose transcendence they understood in essentially Platonic terms. How could that eternal and changeless God be also the God so actively involved in the particularities of redemptive history? The primary difficulty was located in the being of God: was such action compatible with the changelessness of God? So it was a struggle to clarify their understanding of the nature of God that dominated the theological endeavours of the early church and in time gave birth to the Christian doctrine of the Trinity.

That, in broadest outline, was the general form in which the difficulty was primarily felt by most early Christian thinkers. But for most modern Christian thinkers the difficulty is located at a different point. There is a greater readiness to speak in a relatively direct way of the personal nature of God. And to be an agent is a primary feature of personal being. But the various forms of scientific study which dominate our culture have done much to disclose patterns of regularity in the way the world functions. The world as we experience it appears to us a much more regularly ordered world than it did to our predecessors in the faith. Our difficulty in conceiving of God's action is more likely to be focussed on how and where that action is to be located or identified within the world of human experience. The problematic character of God's action remains; the way in which the difficulty is primarily experienced is different.

The contrast that I have drawn is, it must be emphasized, a very broad generalization. Many qualifications would be called for in any more detailed account of it. Some of these at least will, I hope, emerge later as the course of the argument develops. But if not over pressed, the general contrast is, I believe, valid and not unimportant. It might seem at first hearing to be evidence of a masochistic perversity in theologians. If the difficulty comes to be felt less acutely (though certainly still felt) in relation to the being of God, the theologian proceeds to emphasize more strongly the difficulties in relation to the experience of the world. But this is the fruit neither of perversity nor, to go to the other extreme, of chance. It is inherent in the nature of religion. For what is felt to be religiously important is always closely related to what men and women are conscious of lacking in the experience of their lives. Thus we tend to emphasize in our understanding of God what is particularly problematical for us. Where death, disease and natural disaster are frequent and little understood features of human existence, faith is liable to stress the contrasting character of God as wholly removed from all such change and suffering. But where such occurrences are seen rather as part of an inexorable and impersonal law of the universe, then it is God's character as free, personal being that is most firmly apprehended and insisted on by the person of faith. Thus the difficulties that are felt at any one time will never be identical with those that have been most felt in the past, but will always have subtle elements of similarity and dissimilarity in relation to them. Human understanding of God's relation to the world will, and should always expect to, have about it an aspect of standing over against the wisdom of its day. Any religious tradition which does not acknowledge difficulty in the formulation of its faith is the poorer for that fact both religiously and intellectually. A faith that is not hard to hold on to is worth little, but the process of 'holding on' requires continued wrestling with the difficulties that make that faith hard to hold on to. As the early Fathers grappled with their difficulties in the understanding of God's nature, so we need to grapple with the question: Does God act in the world? And, if so, in what ways and by what means?

Traditional Christian teaching about God's action in the world takes a variety of forms. Central are the claims about God's action in the person of Christ, while miracle is frequently emphasized as the most dramatic and most problematic example of such action. But the all-encompassing range of God's more hidden providential activity, which is the essential background to the affirmation of any more specific claims about particular divine actions (whether miraculous or not), is every bit as important and poses problems every bit as acute. I have chosen to raise this broader question first, and will be concentrating on it in the first part of this book, before turning to the more distinctively Christian claims about the person of Christ, because apart from that broader question the more specific claims about Christ cannot even be coherently formulated, let alone appropriately discussed.

An important aspect of the problematic character of this broader concept of God's providential direction of history is the question of intelligibility. God's activity is asserted to be operative on a universal scale. But its relation to the finite activities within the created order has to be affirmed in radically differing forms. God is dissociated from the evil in a way that is claimed to remove all divine responsibility for it, while being so intimately associated with the good as to be the proper recipient of all gratitude and praise. In order to mark those differences, sophisticated forms of appropriate linguistic distinctions were developed. But doubts about how cogently those linguistic distinctions can be made to fit the confused pattern of evil and good in human history are not easily met. And where this conviction of God's general providential guidance is related to specifically Christian history and Christian experience, there is an added dimension to the problem: that concerns the relation between divine grace and human freedom. In the history of Christian thought the intention to do justice to both is almost always in evidence. The successful achievement of that intention is less clear.

These problems are still with us. But they impinge on us in distinctive ways. I spoke earlier of the heart of the contemporary problem as 'likely to be focussed on how and where God's action is to be located and identified within the world of human experience'. Those two words, 'location' and 'identification', may serve to indicate two major features of our contemporary situation. The undeniable advances in historical and scientific knowledge have been achieved by setting on one side any appeal to divine agency. It can rightly be argued that that is only a methodological assumption necessary for practical purposes, and does not necessarily involve any rejection of divine agency as such. Historical and scientific studies do not provide us with the whole truth about the world. What they disclose is valid only within the limitations inherent in their own assumptions as scholarly disciplines. Nevertheless their evident success and the validity, even if limited, of their findings do not leave the position unaltered. Christians in the past have had difficulty enough in trying to relate God's claimed activity to the physical and historical events of the world. The already problematic character of such attempts is increased by our fuller understanding of the ordered patterns of the natural world and of history. The possibility of affirming divine activity is not ruled out, but its specific location is still harder to detect.

The advances in knowledge of which I have just been speaking were dependent on the abandonment of another traditional appeal as well as the appeal to divine agency. That was the appeal to authoritative sources of belief, which were thought to require careful exposition rather than critical assessment. Throughout the greater part of Christian history it has been possible to assume that, whatever the difficulties in interpreting contemporary events, certain events in the past could be known without question to be special divine acts. That knowledge was directly given by the authoritative revelation of scripture. The vigorous intellectual activity that characterized the continuing process of reflection was designed not to determine whether they were divine acts – that was not in question – but how. Appeals to traditional sources as such are not, of course, ruled out for us. They are essential to historical and other forms of knowledge. Indeed we may properly approach them with an *a priori* expectation in their favour; but they can make no absolute claim on our acceptance. Even in the case of scripture, appeal can no longer take the direct, authoritative form that it took so often in the past. Thus not even the most hallowed example of claimed divine action can be accepted as something whose distinctively divine status is directly given; it has to establish its credentials. In this sense the initial identification of what might constitute instances of divine action, as well as their more specific location, is increasingly problematic.

But to be problematic is not to be impossible. It is rather a powerful stimulus to serious theological work. And recent decades have seen considerable attention given to this question of divine action. The work that has been done has taken various forms. The two most obvious forms are biblical and philosophical reflection. Each is indispensable, but neither on its own, nor even the two together, can do the full theological job that is called for. But before we go on to consider how their contribution needs to be supplemented, we must take brief note of the nature of the work that has been done in those two fields.

A stress on the acts of God as the fundamental category for any properly Christian reflection on the nature of God was a leading feature of the 'biblical theology' movement of some thirty years ago. It found symbolic expression in the title of a book by G. E. Wright published in 1952: *God Who Acts*.[6] As a description of a primary feature of the biblical writings, even if one that finds it a little difficult to know what to do with the Wisdom literature, no serious fault need be found with that title. What subsequent work has tended to show is that, however central to the Old Testament the idea of historical events as divine revelation may be, it is nothing like as distinctive a trait as the older tradition of 'biblical theology' had thought. It is, in the words of Bertil Albrektson, 'part of the common theology of the ancient Near East'.[7] That fact does not remove its significance for the Christian theologian altogether, but it raises a question as to how direct or absolute that significance may be.

Philosophical concentration on the theme in the 1960s was partly a reaction to the claims of the biblical theologians, as is witnessed by the title of an article by a professor of philosophy, Frank Dilley: 'Does the "God who acts" really act?'.[8] A series of articles at that time, with titles like 'What sense does it make to say "God acts in history"?'[9] or 'On the meaning of Act of God',[10] aimed to achieve some conceptual clarity about what was meant by such language. Much subsequent writing has continued to pursue that objective in similar vein, drawing particularly on more recent work in the philosophy of action.

These two areas of study are both essential preliminaries to the work of the theologian, but they do not render the theologian's task unnecessary. For Christian theology is not simply a matter of testing the intelligibility of biblical concepts, and reaffirming them when they pass that test. The theologian has to be concerned not only with the biblical roots of the faith that he or she is seeking to understand, but also with how that faith has been developed and understood in the course of Christian history. He has to satisfy himself not only that the traditional claims of that faith are intellectually coherent in themselves, but that they constitute the most appropriate way of understanding the whole range of our human experience and practice.

But if the theological task is as alarmingly wide as that description asserts (and I do not believe it can in the end be more narrowly drawn, however much particular pieces of theological work may rightly set themselves far narrower goals), it is incumbent on the theologian setting out on it to give some account of how it is to be assayed.

No theologian, any more than the proponent of any other scholarly discipline, starts from scratch. However radical his inclinations or intentions, he is heir to a tradition without which he could not even embark on his scholarly task. We have to acknowledge the contingency of the tradition within which we stand. We inherit a vocabulary, patterns of images, categories of thought and established traditions of interpretation. The basic language of our discipline comes to us as something given. This fact has led some theologians to speak of that language and its images as specially given by God and thereby uniquely empowered to express the truth about God. I hold back from speaking of it in this way as a 'revealed' language. To emphasize, as I have done, that its givenness is a givenness from the past is not to rule out some further sense in which it may be said to be given by God. What it does exclude is the idea that there is something demonstrably unique about the manner of its origin or that its givenness is recognizably different from the givenness of other forms of human language or cultural tradition. It does not have a privileged status which confers on it or on particular parts of it immunity from criticism or change. This denial of anything radically different about the origins or status of our Christian language is not to be understood to imply a grudging attitude towards it. It is not simply a matter of there being no serious alternative starting-point for theological reflection. The view that I am outlining is fully compatible with a thoroughly positive attitude, which values the language of Christian tradition for the way it has served and continues to serve as the vehicle of genuine faith. Indeed it is important to remember that the tradition itself has normally acknowledged that however effective a vehicle of faith its language may be, it is always an imperfect vehicle. The intellectual difficulties with which it has had to wrestle throughout its history are witness to that fact.

The basic reason for the imperfection of the language is clear enough. If we are using finite, human language to speak of a transcendent God, it cannot be other than an imperfect vehicle. From the earliest days of the church, many of her theologians have expressed the reluctance with which they have felt constrained to articulate truths that lie beyond the range of human speech. It is important to recognize that theology is something that can only properly exist on the other side of silence. Even if Bultmann's rejection of the use of any language directly about God as a form of false objectivization may be overstated, the claim of a theologian like Austin Farrer that our language can only function as a distant analogue in its reference to God is surely justified.[11] But there is a second reason also, whose recognition, though not its operation, belongs more exclusively to recent times. Language and ideas do not exist in a vacuum. They are an integral part of the culture and the world-view of their time. Changes in culture and world-view cannot leave religious language unaffected. They do not make the old language wholly inaccessible or powerless. But they stimulate change, sometimes conscious sometimes unconscious, in relation both to the language and to the ideas. The process is never easy. But it is both inevitable and proper. Modern historical and sociological study has not created this phenomenon, but it has made us more aware of its operation both now and in the past. In the light of that greater awareness we should be in a better position to combine a positive attitude to Christian tradition with the recognition that such an attitude does not mean that we ought simply to take it over without change. Just as it has in fact gone through substantial modification in the past, so it still calls for continuing modification today through interaction with our experience.

'Experience' is a crucial but highly problematic concept. It is not some raw stuff that can be set over against tradition as something wholly independent of it, and therefore able to function as a wholly distinct element in the interaction of which I have just spoken. What we experience is intimately affected by the intellectual and religious tradition within which we stand. But it is not simply an epiphenomenon of that tradition either. It is not wholly determined by it, and can therefore properly contribute to its modification. Within the broad category of 'experience' various distinctions can be drawn. One basic distinction is that between lived experience and formal reasoning. Both can play an influential role in prompting the modification of earlier beliefs. In relation to God's action in the world, a primary motivation for a modified account may be that many people do not any longer experience what happens to them in the world in those terms in the way that they used to do. Alternatively, the primary motivation for a changed view may be that earlier reasoned accounts of how God's action is to be understood in relation to secondary causation in the world no longer appear as intellectually convincing as once they did. A combination of practical and theoretical changes of this kind can rightly contribute to the modification of past tradition, sometimes in quite extensive ways.

At a formal level, there is a comparatively close parallel with the development of science. The scientist too inherits a scientific orthodoxy without which he could not function as a scientist at all. That orthodoxy includes both a number of widely agreed beliefs, and a language, including a standard selection of models, in terms of which those beliefs are expressed. There is even an element of contingency about the selection of the theoretical models the scientist employs. They are not self-evidently the only models that could have been used. Their choice may sometimes have been influenced sociologically, by for example the technological needs of a particular society at a particular time. This inherited orthodoxy, in the form both of its agreed beliefs and of its models, is always subject to modification, by interaction with experience. That experience may take a primarily practical form. Life is no longer perceived as the prevailing orthodoxy suggests it should be. New experiments do not work out as expected. But it may also take a more theoretical form. Old theories may come to seem clumsy and unsatisfying. Tidier formulations are worked out to take their place. Motivations of both kinds work together to effect a continuous process of modification to the prevailing pattern of scientific beliefs.

That process, though continuous, is not uniform. A moment may come which calls for a particularly drastic alteration of the old picture. The accepted model of the sun revolving round the earth has to give way to one of the earth going round the sun. The appropriate moment for such a change is not self-evident. For a time it may be possible, and may well seem better, to accommodate the new experiences with appropriate and ever-increasing alterations to the old picture. But there comes a point at which a shift of paradigm becomes the only appropriate response. Theology is even more reluctant to embrace such far-reaching changes for two reasons. The necessarily ana-logical nature of its language means that it has a flexibility of interpretation more akin to that of literature than to that of science. The alternative strategy of modifying the sense in which the old language is to be understood can be more readily sustained there than in the scientific parallel. Moreover the language of theology is closely related to the practice of faith, and the repercussions of major shifts in language and belief are not easily accommodated at that level. There is therefore a proper pressure towards conservatism in theology. Nevertheless what we may call the two strategies of revisionism (modification of detail of belief and shift of basic paradigm) both have a place in theology, as in other areas of knowledge. There comes a time when any further stretching of the old language becomes too great and cannot honestly reflect the intended changes in sensibility. Some more far-reaching change of underlying image or conceptuality is required. It is called for both by the changes in lived experience and in reasoned reflection. It is needed in the service both of faith and of reason.

The problems posed by the questions 'Does God act in the world? And if so, in what ways, and by what means?' are of such magnitude that it seems highly probable that some significant shift away from traditional answers to those questions may be called for. Indeed, we cannot rule out in advance that what is called for may prove to be some even bigger shift in conceptuality in relation to the underlying notion of divine agency itself.

2

God the Creator

'I believe in God the Father almighty, maker of heaven and earth and of all things visible and invisible.' The famous debates and controversies that mark the early history of Christian thought were largely concerned with the understanding of the person of Christ, spelt out in the much longer second clause of the creed. We are inclined by way of contrast to think of the first clause with its affirmation of God as creator as little more than a tautology. Certainly the main Christian tradition has not only maintained it without hesitation but has laid great stress on the absoluteness of the work of creation as creation *ex nihilo*.

Yet the firmness of this insistence is in some respects surprising. Such an understanding of creation was certainly not seen as a straightforward or self-evident truth from the beginning. The idea is not explicitly affirmed in scripture. The question had not been formulated at that stage in a way that called for a conscious judgment one way or the other on the issue. Nor did it seem the most natural interpretation of scripture to some of the earliest Christian writers. Platonists at the time, developing the model of the craftsman from the *Timaeus*, saw the work of creation as giving form to the shapeless, pre-existent stuff out of which the world was made. For Justin Martyr the evidence of scripture pointed in the same direction. He quotes Gen. 1.2, 'The earth was without form and void, and darkness was upon the face of the earth; and the spirit of God was moving upon the face of the waters', and, seeing this as a picture of the work of creation, he goes on to comment on the text in these words:

> So by God's word the whole universe was made out of this substratum of which Moses speaks – and Plato and the Platonists have learned it from him.[1]

Like many a later theologian, he rejoices to find scripture and the wisdom of his day apparently at one. What better confirmation could he want of an understanding of creation as the giving of form to formless matter? And when a little later on Christian writers began to make explicit assertion of the idea of creation out of nothing, the lack of clear scriptural backing for that position was something of an embarrassment. Tertullian is reduced to the sophistical argument of claiming that since scripture says nothing about that from which the world is made, it must indeed have been made from nothing.[2] And Origen, most assiduous of all searchers of scripture, is constrained to offer as his supporting scriptural evidence two texts, one from II Maccabees and one from the Shepherd of Hermas.[3]

More significant than the absence of any explicit affirmation of the idea in scripture is the fact that it adds gravely to the most serious challenge that the theist has to face, namely the problem of evil. For if we understand creation as the shaping of recalcitrant raw material for which God is not ultimately responsible rather than as the origination not only of form but of matter itself, then we seem to have at least the beginnings of a path away from the ascription of ultimate responsibility for that evil to God himself, which the notion of creation out of nothing appears to involve. Nor, as creation out of nothing began to take its place as an accepted part of Christian teaching, were Christians unaware of this implication of what they were affirming. Difficulty in accounting for the origin of evil in the world was an important aspect of the motivation of the Gnostics and Marcionites, over against whom Tertullian and Origen first gave the idea of creation out of nothing clear Christian formulation. And the same difficulty continues to be an important part of the motivation that has led some contemporary theologians also to challenge this traditional Christian doctrine. Process theologians may still, like Justin Martyr, appeal for support to Plato and the Old Testament,[4] but the religious and philosophical help it appears to offer to Christian reflection on evil is a far more significant reason for their criticism of the traditional teaching.[5] Behind their challenge lies the Whiteheadian conviction that 'the object of authentic religious concern is characterized more decisively by goodness than by metaphysical ultimacy'.[6] In terms of the theological method that I outlined in the previous chapter, the doctrine of creation out of nothing must indeed seem a strong candidate for radical modification.

Nevertheless it seems to me clear that there can be no going back on that conviction for the Christian theologian. In my judgment it is both philosophically and religiously essential. Creation is creation out of nothing or it is nothing. An indispensable element in any contemporary defence of theistic belief is the sense of mystery as to how it comes about that there is anything at all. Much more than that is needed for the establishment and practice of Christian faith. But without it a reasonable faith seems to be an impossibility. If God is not the source of all existence, then he is a dispensable hypothesis within our finite world and must take his chance of survival along with the other explanatory hypotheses spawned by the fertile human mind. Religiously also the idea of God as absolute creator would appear to be necessary to that form of religious experience which finds in God its 'final succour and absolute demand'.[7] If it is right to see 'finality' and 'absoluteness' as integral to Christian experience, they too point towards a God who is absolute creator. If that doctrine cannot stand, then the case for a rational Christian theism is seriously undermined and the nature of any alternative form of Christian faith would be reduced to a pale shadow.

But the difficulties to which the doctrine has given rise have been real enough, and bold language of the kind that I have been using will not make them go away. I have already referred to process theology as giving contemporary expression to a reasoned criticism of the doctrine. The objections it puts forward need to be taken seriously. The heart of those objections is summed up in the complaint that the 'doctrine (of *creatio ex nihilo*) is part and parcel of the doctrine of God as absolute controller'.[8] In the view of its critics, the traditional understanding of the absolute sovereignty of God as creator does not leave room for genuine contingency or genuine independence on the part of created reality. If that is in fact the case, it was, as I suggested in the last chapter, certainly not the intention of the leading exponents of that earlier Christian tradition. But there is much in that tradition to lend credence to the process theologian's complaint.

Let me begin by taking the most notable (one is tempted to say the most notorious) example of a distinguished theologian whose work gives rise to such objections. John Calvin begins his discussion of creation by insisting that 'it were cold and lifeless to represent God as a momentary creator who completed his work once for all, and then left it'.[9] The doctrine is just as much concerned with God's continued governance of heaven and earth by a providence which 'so overrules all things that nothing happens without his counsel'.[10] This overruling control of God is universal in its scope. 'By his providence, not heaven and earth and inanimate creatures only, but also the counsels and wills of men are so governed as to move exactly in the course which he has destined'.[11] It is not enough to speak only of a general or universal providence, for that would not 'prevent man from turning himself in this direction or in that, according to the mere freedom of his own will'.[12] Nor, even in the case of evil actions, is it sufficient to speak of God's permissive will. Even in those cases God is agent, not simply in terms of a 'universal agency of God which, as it sustains all creatures, also gives them all their power of acting', but in terms also of 'that special agency which is apparent in every act'.[13]

In taking Calvin as my first example of Christian teaching, I have of course chosen an extreme example of insistence on God's predestinating control of both human history and the human heart. But as we shall see clearly enough when we come to look more fully later on at the general character of Christian teaching about divine providence, many a Christian teacher (who would strongly repudiate Calvin's full-blooded predestinarian views) has found himself having to work in practice with a somewhat similar picture of God's control of the world of nature and of men and women. Furthermore, the basic framework of Calvin's thought in terms of the coincidence of divine and human agency within what we experience as a single action finds classic expression in the earlier teaching of Aquinas. And even that more moderate and representative form of Christian teaching is not free of the difficulties which process theology levels against the main Christian tradition.

For Aquinas also the essential meaning of creation concerned not the origin of the world but its continuing dependence on God. He did in fact believe on the basis of revelation that the world was not eternal but had a beginning in time, but that was a contingent fact. It could have been eternal without altering in any way the absoluteness of the ontological dependence of creature on creator, which is what creation is. God as creator is the primary cause of our existence and we are dependent on him for the power of being. But the world is not a world only of existents; it is a world of agents. God is therefore to be seen also as the primary cause of all action. As we are dependent on him for the power of being, so are we also for the power of acting. Secondary causes, both inanimate and human, have a real but only relative independence. God is always present as the primary cause enabling them to act. Aquinas' main emphasis is on the reality rather than on the subordinate status of the secondary cause. He argues vigorously against those who would deny reality to finite causes. Nevertheless the overall control or governance of divine causation is never in question. 'Everything God wills comes about.'[14] Admittedly it does not all come about in precisely the same way. 'What the plan of divine providence has arranged to result necessarily and without fail will come about necessarily and without fail; what too it has arranged to result contingently will come about contingently.'[15] Secondary causes have their own reality, therefore, and human causes their freedom. But if that affirmation is to be taken seriously, as it must, it is difficult to know what sense to give to the concept of an arranged contingency. Certainly it is a closely confined degree of freedom that is being asserted. When Aquinas declares that 'although one whom God reprobates cannot gain grace, nevertheless the fact that he flounders in this or that sin happens of his own free will',[16] how much consolation is contained in the qualifying clause? Some modification of the language or of the conceptuality that has led Christians to speak in such terms does seem to be called for.

In its attempt to provide an alternative conceptuality, which will avoid all such unwelcome implications of God's sovereignty, how far has process theology felt the need to modify the doctrine of creation out of nothing? In the thought of Whitehead, which is the primary inspiration of the process school, what is most ultimate is creativity, and God can be described as its 'accident' or 'outcome' or 'creature'.[17] What the precise relation between the two was for Whitehead has been the subject of intense debate; but that need not concern us here. For later process theologians, like John Cobb, have been concerned not simply to reproduce Whitehead's ideas but rather to make use of his fundamental insights in order to develop their own more explicitly Christian account of God as creator. For John Cobb creativity does exist independently of God, yet it is more an abstraction or a principle than some entity standing over against God. It may be envisaged as a kind of chaos or random flux, but it has neither the permanence nor the directionality that would enable us to speak of it as an entity or thing of any kind – until the formative influence of God upon it has given it such permanence and directionality. Thus John Cobb can still assert that God is 'the reason that entities occur at all'.[18] If we stress the final word sufficiently, we can even say that for him creation is out of no *thing*. For John Cobb, then, there is a departure from the full traditional doctrine of creation *ex nihilo*, but the modification is less drastic than might have been expected. And David Pailin, the foremost British exponent of process thought, goes a stage further in the same direction. He argues that even Whitehead's remarks about God as the 'creature' or 'accident' of creativity 'need not be developed so as to deny the ultimacy of God'.

> It is not that God is subject to creativity as if creativity existed prior to God and 'produced' God. Rather, the situation is that to be God is necessarily to be creative.[19]

On that understanding conflict with the main thrust of the traditional doctrine, as opposed to ways in which it has at times been understood or to corollaries that have been thought to follow from it, seems to have reached vanishing point.

In the light of these reflections the question that I want to raise is whether any modification of the doctrine of creation out of nothing is in fact needed to order to achieve the laudable religious objectives which the process theologian is concerned to establish. Is it the only way to avoid an unacceptable doctrine of God the absolute controller? But I do not intend to develop my own proposal in direct dialogue with process thought. I have discussed process theology's objection to creation *ex nihilo*, because it represents the most serious and sustained contemporary challenge to that doctrine. But my positive proposal, while seeking to be sensitive to those objections, does not need to be expressed in Whiteheadian or process terms. It can equally well be put in the more traditional categories of the Thomistic scheme. Must the God who is the power of all being also be the power of all acting? The tradition has insisted that God gives to created realities their natural capacities for action but that they can only operate those capacities as they are moved by God. Why should it not be the case that God has bestowed on created realities not only their natural capacities for action but also the power to move themselves to action independently of specific divine agency in each case? Or, to put the point more generally still, is the idea of God's absolute creation out of nothing compatible with the assertion that God may have conferred on parts at least of his creation a genuine independence of agency in relation to himself?

In approaching that question, I want to begin by recalling another feature of the initial formation of the doctrine, to which I have not yet explicitly referred. I spoke earlier of the doctrine of creation out of nothing as established over against the alternative of a metaphysical dualism, which had its roots in one aspect of Plato's thought and which found expression at the time in some forms of Gnosticism and later on in Manichaean teaching. But that was not the only alternative to a doctrine of creation out of nothing. There was another way of depicting the world as causally dependent upon God, which pictured the world as an emanation from the One or from God, like light coming out from the sun or water from the fountain. This was the approach developed by Plotinus and the Neo-platonists. But the church had no hesitation in deciding against such a picture and opting for the idea of creation, understood as an act of divine will. Two main arguments were adduced in support of that preference. In the first place the lack of conscious purpose implicit in the model of emanation suggested the idea of some external necessity imposed upon God. God, according to that model, does not choose to create a world; creation is something that apparently happens to God willy-nilly. It was felt, therefore, to do less justice than the other account to the concept of God's transcendence. And secondly, the model did not depict the world as sufficiently distinct from God. There is a sense in which the light is a part of the sun, the water simply an extension of the fountain. The world envisaged in that way might still be dependent on God, but it appeared to be too nearly a part of him for a religious consciousness rooted in the Christian scriptures.

If then we conceive of creation in terms of an act of divine will rather than of an emanation from God, there does not seem to be any fundamental conceptual difficulty in affirming that God could have created a world with the kind of independence of himself which I have postulated. For if creation is both absolute and a matter of will, then the form that it takes is restricted only by the law of non-contradiction. And that of course is no restriction at all, since what contradicts the law of non-contradiction is no alternative possibility but merely a form of words without sense or meaning. We may have no experience of creating something which has complete freedom of action in relation to us its creator; but there is nothing self-contradictory in the notion. If that argument is valid, then it is not the affirmation of such a divine self-limitation in the act of creation but the denial of its possibility that would represent a qualification of the absoluteness of God's creative work. In a memorable phrase of Karl Barth, it would be to make God 'the prisoner of his own power'.[20]

The proposal that I am making involves, therefore, no denial of God's omnipotence, no reduction in the affirmation of divine power. What it does involve is a modification of the way in which the concept of that power is understood. That point has been well put in a recent book by Thomas Tracy. 'God,' he writes,

> creates a field of other agents whose integrity he respects and so whose independent actions condition his choices. This amounts to a purposeful limitation of the scope of his own activity, but it does not nullify his omnipotence . . . Intentional self-restraint does not represent a renunciation of omnipotence, but rather a renunciation of certain uses of power.[21]

Tracy is surely right to emphasize the polyvalence of the concept of power in the context of personal relations. A powerful monarch may wield power over his kingdom by the strength of his army and the rigour of his laws. A powerful business magnate may exercise his power by skilful manipulation or outmanoeuvring of subordinates and rivals alike. But the powerful advocate of a cause may achieve his goals by winning the hearts and minds of so many people that they freely combine to work for the desired end. The last of those three may seem furthest away from the operation of power at the purely physical level, which we are inclined to regard as the basic and truest meaning of the word 'power'. But it is also the most morally praiseworthy and the most difficult to achieve. If the picture of creation which we are led to develop involves that conception of God's power in relation to human action, that fact should be seen not as a weakness but as an argument in its favour.

The same fundamental point may be made in a slightly different way. I have been speaking so far in terms of a modification of the understanding of God's power. One could speak instead of a qualification of the concept of power by that of love. It is in this form that the point is made by another recent writer, Grace Jantzen. She writes:

> The proper order of priority in understanding the attributes of God must be to take his love as central, and modify our ideas of omnipotence . . . in terms of it . . . Creative love is love which gives autonomy to that which it creates; and though omnipotence can be limited by nothing else, it is limited by love . . . If God's power is understood as the expression of his love, then God's power is his power to give independence, autonomy, even to creatures over whom, strictly speaking, he is sovereign.[22]

Conceptually there may be disadvantages in speaking of one attribute of God having priority over another. It runs the risk of suggesting some kind of tension within the being of God. Nevertheless religiously there are compensating gains in the vividness with which the main point can be conveyed. This is powerfully expressed in some words of Sören Kierkegaard:

> O wonderful omnipotence and love! A man cannot bear that his 'creations' should be something directly over against him; they should be nothing and therefore he calls them creations with contempt. But God, who creates out of nothing, who almightily takes from nothing and says 'Be!' lovingly adds 'Be something even over against me'. Wonderful love, even his omnipotence is under the power of love.

Hence the reciprocal relationship. If God were only the almighty, there would be no reciprocal relation; for the creation is nothing for the Almighty. But it is something for love.[23]

What that quotation from Kierkegaard helps to make clear is that the account of creation that I am proposing is not one called for by human pride, determined to defend at all costs its own autonomy; it is one called for by religious faith, concerned to establish the reality of what Kierkegaard calls our 'reciprocal relation' with God. That same motivation has played an important role also in process theology's critique of traditional views. Charles Hartshorne, indeed, after Whitehead the founder figure of process thought, uses the same language of reciprocity. He writes:

Religion is concerned with interaction between creator and creatures, not with mere action by the one upon the others. Examine any basic aspect of religious practice. It will exhibit divine-human reciprocity as essential.[24]

And that is something which in his view traditional theology, as embodied in Thomistic thought, is unable to provide. Aquinas' concern to safeguard the self-sufficiency of God leads him to give careful qualification to the idea of divine-human reciprocity. God's self-giving cannot involve his essential nature. In the technical language of Aquinas' theological scheme, God's relation to us is conceptual not real.[25]

The concerns that give rise to the linguistic caution that Aquinas displays in this regard cannot be lightly brushed aside. Christians are right to want to speak of a reciprocal relation, and of a God who feels our sorrows, is grieved by our sins and responds to our prayers and our love. But we cannot responsibly do so, as some contemporary theologians appear to do, by simply affirming the passibility of God, as if the ancient insistence of God's unchangingness and impassibility were just a foolish mistake to be denied outright. There is an important truth implicit in that old conviction. It is the truth that God is never, as we are, affected by forces or events which come entirely from outside the sphere of his own influence. The proposal that I am making takes note of that ancient and proper insistence. If God is affected by us or 'suffers' because of what we do, that is not the result of something that has happened wholly apart from God. As creator he has chosen to create a world of free beings with that measure of independent power over against himself.

That is the understanding of God as creator which I wish to propose. In subsequent chapters I shall try to see what difference it makes to related areas of Christian reflection. What alleviation, if any, does it offer to the Christian's attempt to come to terms with the problem of evil? What modification does it call for in the understanding of providence? But before we embark on such questions, a further clarification is called for in the basic understanding of creation here proposed. I began by giving voice to a general disquiet about the idea of divine agency, about how and where God acts in the world. So I propose next to consider more precisely how the idea of creation I have outlined is itself best understood and spoken of in terms of God's action.

3

The Creation and God's Action

In the previous chapter I offered a defence of the traditional Christian doctrine of creation as creation *ex nihilo*. But I sought at the same time to dissociate myself from the strong doctrine of divine providential control of the detailed happenings within the world that has so often accompanied it in traditional Christian teaching. Instead I put a strong emphasis on the radical degree of freedom of action with which I believe the human creation to have been endowed. Whatever account of divine agency we finally offer must be consistent with the evident fact that we are agents, capable of effective and responsible action, contributing to what happens in our world.

How then can we best understand and speak of God's relation to this world of his creation? The brief and indirect attention I have so far given to that topic needs more careful elaboration. In the last chapter I made positive, if somewhat uncritical, use of two traditional ideas. I accepted that the fundamental nature of creation itself was best understood as an act of divine will; and I spoke of a reciprocal divine-human relationship as a religious reality for which any appropriate understanding of creation must leave room. But neither of those two ideas has stood unqualified or unquestioned within the tradition itself, nor is either free from those contemporary difficulties about divine action of which I am trying to take particular account.

The idea of creation as an act of divine will may have won out over the alternative idea of emanation, but it was not unaffected by it. For if we speak of creation as an act of divine will, we can hardly allow that language to suggest a picture of God deliberating whether or not to create, and somehow weighing up the relative advantages and disadvantages of particular possible forms of creation. If our aim is to provide the most truly personal conception of God's work of creation that we can envisage, the alternative emanationist picture may have something of importance to offer. For conscious deliberation is not a necessary mark of the most profoundly personal actions at the human level. We value the spontaneous generosity that flows naturally from the kind of person the agent is more highly than the nicely calculated less or more of the conscientious but emotionally detached giver. Thus that which naturally flows out of a person may offer a more, and not a less, personal image of action than that which is the outcome of conscious deliberation and choice. So the two images have come to influence one another. Though it was creation that emerged as the only acceptable concept, in the long run it was an understanding of creation substantially changed from that suggested by talk of an act of will. As Aquinas was to insist, the work of creation is best seen as the natural overflow of God's goodness.[1] If that picture is to be described as incorporating an element of necessity, it is a kind of necessity that we commend at the human level. It is no externally imposed necessity, but one that springs from within the nature of the agent. It is the mark of the saint who is unable to act other than out of love.

Nor is the conception of a reciprocal relation between human persons and God the only model of profound religious experience within the Christian tradition. God may have spoken to Moses face to face as a man speaks with his friend; but God also met with Moses in the thick darkness on the summit of Mount Sinai.[2] And that entering of Moses into the deep darkness at the top of the mount has become an important symbol within one strand of Christian mysticism, where 'reciprocal relationship' would be an unnatural terminology to describe the experience affirmed.

It is important to recall the degree to which these more straightforwardly personalist images of God's relationship to his creation have been qualified in the past, as we take up our own particular quest: how is the idea of God's action most appropriately used in the context of our proposed understanding of creation? An action is to be distinguished from a mere happening or accident. We cannot always tell just by observation whether what we have witnessed is act or accident. A car swerves off the road and over a cliff. We may not be able to discover whether it was a deliberate act of suicide or the accident of either an exhausted driver fallen asleep or a mechanical failure of the brakes – or yet again whether, if the driver's drink had been drugged or the brake cables deliberately cut, it might be an act, but the act of someone not even present at the scene of the happening. An act always involves an intention and a goal. Billiard balls banging into one another do not as such constitute an 'act'. They only do so if they are part of an act of potting, with a human intention of making one of the balls fall into a pocket. To call something an 'act', then, is to give a unity to what would otherwise appear only as random occurrences, and to do so by bringing them together as contributory to some overall intention.

With this understanding of action in mind, the proposal that I want to make is that the primary usage for the idea of divine action should be in relation to the world as a whole rather than to particular occurrences within it. Preliminary support for this proposal can be found in the final chapter of John McMurray's book, *The Self as Agent*. For he claims there that 'the only way in which we can conceive our experience as a whole is by thinking of the world as one action'.[3] The category of action, he argues, is more fundamental than that of process. For action can incorporate process, but not the other way round. The unifying intentionality which is the distinctive and constitutive feature of 'action' cannot be fully brought within the idea of an ongoing process. 'It is therefore *possible*,' McMurray concludes, 'to think the world as one action. It is *not possible* to think it as a unitary process.'[4]

So for the theist, who is necessarily committed to a unitary view of the world, the whole process of the bringing into being of the world, which is still going on, needs to be seen as one action of God. This idea has been firmly enunciated by a number of contemporary theologians. Thus Gordon Kaufman writes:

> For a monotheistic theology . . . it is *the whole course of history* from its initiation in God's creative activity to its consummation when God ultimately achieves his purposes, that should be conceived as God's act in the primary sense.[5]

And John Hick has written in a similar vein:

> The most basic and general conception of an action, as we use the word in relation to humanity and as we may apply it analogously in relation to deity, is that of an event enacting an agent's intention. In this basic sense God's continuous creation/salvation of the world is his action.[6]

If we adopt this view, as I believe we should, two questions follow:

1. Does speaking of the world as a whole as a single act of God inhibit our use of the language of God's agency in relation to more specific occurrences within the world? And if we are to speak of God as agent in these other more limited respects also, how are those actions of God to be understood in relation to the one overarching action of God of which they form a part?

2. Can we characterize this single act of God in some more specific way? Since actions are of many kinds, we need to ask whether there are particular types of action which are specially appropriate analogues of this one fundamental act of God.

The first question is one that will continue as a major concern throughout this book. Important aspects of it lie at the heart of the discussions of providence and grace to which we shall be coming later. I propose to leave until that stage, therefore, any consideration of that whole range of activity in which human intentionality is involved. At this stage I want to take up only the question of whether we should speak of divine agency in relation to particular physical occurrences at the non-intelligent level. The distinction that I am drawing here is not entirely straightforward. Unless we are extreme dualists in our understanding of the human person, there is always an important physical element in every historical and personal occasion. Nevertheless it is a distinction that we naturally do make and can quite properly make, if we do not thereby imply an absolute separation between the two.

In one respect this aspect of the question, in which our concern is only with the physical or natural world, would seem to be the easier part of the task. Since by definition we are concerned with occurrences where no human intentionality is involved, we are not faced with the issue of two, possibly conflicting, intentionalities in relation to the same occurrence. If we are right to speak of 'action' at all in such cases, God would seem to be the only candidate for the role of agent. Nevertheless there are serious difficulties. Traditional Christian understanding has seen the divine intention for the world, which alone justifies our speaking of it as a single act, in terms of the creation of men and women in God's own image and bringing them to their proper fulfilment in a perfect relationship to himself and to one another. If we claimed that as a complete account of the divine intention, we might justly be accused of being unduly anthropocentric. It may be that we need also to speak of intentions in relation to the being of God himself; or there may be other intentions of which we are in no position to know anything. But if we are right to speak of the world as a single intentional act at all, it seems undeniable on any score that human consciousness and human loving must be seen as vital elements in that intention. Thus the purely physical occurrences, with which alone we are concerned at the moment, provide the substructure that serves to make that intention, and therefore the one divine action, possible. Their contribution to that single act is all-pervasive, but in large measure indirect. It is therefore a questionable enterprise to try to speak of God's agency in relation to particular physical occurrences, as if that were something that could be done in even relative separation from the question of their contribution to the one act that constitutes the world as a whole.

The nature of these difficulties may become a little clearer if we consider the very different ways in which the problem has been tackled by three theologians or theological schools in recent times. Bultmann's answer to our question was un-equivocal. No such links can be made at all. To speak of divine agency in relation to purely physical occurrences is neither possible nor permissible. It is important to recognize the reasons for this refusal. It is not a straightforward denial that there may be such links; it is a denial that we are in any position to speak of them. This is because of the radically different ways in which, according to Bultmann and the existentialist tradi-tion, our knowledge of physical occurrences and our knowledge of God are grounded. In the former case our knowledge is built up by a method of study which sets the subject or observer over against the object or thing observed. But that method, however effective in its own sphere, cannot serve as an approach to the knowledge of God. God is not an external reality who can be an object of our observation and therefore of that kind of knowledge. The only way in which God can be known is in and through our experience of him; it is a way that has more in common with the acquisition of knowledge through personal love or poetic insight than with the way in which scientific knowledge of the world is established. The knowledge thus obtained cannot be extrapolated from its given relation to human experience and human existence, and then expressed in a form that would enable us to speak of God's relation to the inanimate order of creation as such. Bultmann speaks for himself as well as for St Paul when he describes Paul's teaching in these terms:

God's creatorship is not, for Paul, a cosmological theory which professes to explain the origin of the world and its existence as it is. Rather, it is a proposition that concerns man's existence . . . Knowledge of God as creator contains primarily knowledge of man – man, that is, in his creatureliness and in his situation of being one to whom God has laid claim.[7]

Bultmann's reluctance to allow any answer to our question must be taken seriously. He can muster some good theological arguments in its support. Nevertheless it cannot be allowed to settle the question. Personal and scientific ways of knowing cannot be as sharply separated off from one another as Bultmann's account of them implies. And it is the absoluteness of the distinction that he believes to exist between them that leads to the absoluteness of his bar against our speaking of God in direct relation to the purely physical occurrences within the world.

By way of contrast, process theology has a strongly unitive approach to knowledge, as is to be expected of a theological tradition which finds its primary inspiration in the scientist-philosopher, Whitehead. It is also, as we saw last time, strongly opposed to any conception of God as absolute controller. God's power is always exercised by way of suasion rather than coercion. Now in relation to the human creation, there is much to be said for such a view, and we shall come back to it in that context in due course. But in process thought there is no fundamental difference between the way God relates to human or historical events and the way he relates to natural processes. There too God as the source of all future possibilities sets before each occasion the possibility of novelty. But this is not coercive or determinative. The outcome depends on the internally determined response of the occasion itself, however rudimentary or lacking in consciousness that occasion may be. The striking nature of this pan-psychic vision of reality is well illustrated by Whitehead's remark that 'the Castle Rock at Edinburgh exists from moment to moment and from century to century, by reason of the decision effected by its own historic route of antecedent occasions'.[8] The implausibility of such language needs no underlining. Yet it has proved attractive to a number of theologians not closely identified with process thought. Thus John Taylor speaks of the Spirit as he 'who

confronts each isolated spontaneous particle with the beck-
oning reality of the larger whole and . . . lures the inert
organisms forward by giving an inner awareness and recognition of the unattained.'[9] The novelty that characterizes the
emergent evolution by which our world has developed is a
mysterious phenomenon. But to try to account for it in terms
of the lure of divine love winning a response from the most
primitive forms of physical existents is to add confusion to
mystery, however carefully the meanings of such words as
'response' and 'awareness' are qualified. The attempt to describe God's action in relation to purely physical phenomena in
such terms lacks all credibility.

Since neither the radically dualistic approach of Rudolf
Bultmann nor the unitary approach of process theology offers
a satisfactory answer to our problem, I turn for my third
example to someone who follows the more traditional approach of primary and secondary causation. In his use of this
traditional schema, Austin Farrer does not wish to mitigate in
any way the traditional stress on God's 'ultimate mastery over
all existence'.[10] But he develops the approach in a way that
takes full cognizance of advances in scientific knowledge. And
this leads him to stress, even more than Aquinas, the genuine
independence of the patterns of causal activity within the
world. Moreover, his understanding of science leads him to
insist that the basic stuff of the created order is not things,
however rudimentary, but energy. And he sees this fact as
highly significant for any attempt to understand the relation
between God and creaturely reality. For it means that there is
no 'comfortable cushion' of created object between the creative activity of God and creaturely energy or activity, since
energy or activity is the most basic form of created reality. 'If
God creates energies, he creates going activities. What he
causes is their acting as they do.'[11] Thus the coexistence of
divine and creaturely action in respect of the same act is not
some further truth to be argued for or against in addition to
the affirmation of divine creation. Since energy or creaturely
activity is the basic form of created reality, the coexistence of

the two distinct forms of activity is already given in the affirmation of divine creation.

> Running oneself one's own way is the same thing as existing. If God had made things to exist, but not to run their own way, he would have made them to exist and not to exist.[12]

Finite existents, then, all do their own things in their own ways. That is what it is to be created. But there is also an analogous divine doing at the same time in relation to those activities. How is this divine doing to be characterized? What kind of intention can be ascribed to it? Farrer takes as an example the difficult case of a natural disaster like the Lisbon earthquake. The answer that he gives has nothing to do with judgment on sin or warnings of mortality, as might have been expected from many of his predecessors in the faith. What he says is:

> The will of God expressed in the event is his will for the physical elements in the earth's crust or under it: his will that they should go on being themselves and acting in accordance with their natures.[13]

So the divine intention in such a case is of a very general kind. God makes the world, as Farrer puts it, 'from the bottom up'.[14] Energy and its physical expression constitute the basic building bricks out of which the whole universe, with all its human and spiritual richness, is constructed. So it is God's will that the physical elements should continue to be themselves and the energies to function in their own way. The divine intention of which Farrer speaks is uniform in the same way that the primary causation of Aquinas' scheme is a uniform enabling of the secondary causes' power to act. Farrer's account does not help us to speak of divine action in relation to particular physical occurrences in a way which adds anything to what is already being said in the affirmation of the whole creative process as God's single intentional action.

What would be the implications of accepting the conclusion that there are no good grounds for speaking of particular divine actions with respect to particular phenomena at the sub-human level? In my view they are remarkably small. That may well seem a surprising judgment, since the difference is often seen as the difference between an unacceptable deism on the one hand and an acceptable theism on the other. For confirmation of it I want to spell out what those implications might be in terms of the two most sharply contrasting models of God's relation to the world that have been characteristic of the history of Christian thought. This will have the added advantage of preparing the way at the same time for moving on to our second question as to what kind of action we should conceive God's act of creation to be.

The first model is that of the craftsman, of the potter and the clay. In the case of the divine analogue the potter has endowed the clay with its distinctive properties. Those properties have become properties of the clay and there does not seem to be any need to relate divine agency directly to the regular manner of their functioning. Divine agency relates rather to the way they ultimately come together to form the one divine act of the creation of the whole as an intentional unity. Such a way of looking at the matter is likely to be rejected as unacceptably deistic. The alternative model, on the other hand, wholly avoids that particular objection. It is the immanentist account, which sees God's relation to the world not as that of a person to some external reality but rather as that of a soul or self to its own body. The physical processes of the world are the means of God's self-expression, as the unconscious physiological functioning of our bodies is for us. Here too it hardly seems natural to speak of divine agency at work, any more than we would speak of the agency of a human self in continually maintaining the pumping activity of the heart. Thus the two apparently contrasting models begin to coalesce. They conflict in their spatial imagery, but not in what they suggest about divine agency at the level of physical occurrence within the world. Both encourage us to see it as part of that ongoing activity which contributes to the one divine act of God's creation; neither encourages us to speak of specific divine action in relation to particular physical occurrences.

At this level, therefore, the difference between a deistic picture according to which the emergent properties of evolving matter are in some sense inherently programmed in advance and a theistic model according to which God is the ever-present, ever-active creator, calling out those emergent properties *in via* is the difference between two alternative imageries, each with its own weaknesses, rather than between two substantially conflicting claims. Thus Hugh Montefiore speaks of the mutation at the heart of the evolutionary process as due to a 'bias implanted in matter' and then goes on to say that 'another way of describing this bias would be to call it the Holy Spirit working within the matter of the universe, unfolding the purposes of the Creator by immanent operation'.[15] The two accounts are used as alternative ways of indicating the same single reality of God's relation to the evolutionary process. Whether the difference between the two will be equally small when we move on to consider the human and the historical sphere remains to be seen.

For the moment, however, we must take up our second question. If it is the creation of the world as a whole that is most appropriately spoken of as God's act, can we characterize the nature of that act more fully in ways that will do justice to our emphasis on the gift of freedom to finite beings as a distinctive feature of that creation? We have just been considering two traditional models, that of the potter and the clay and that of God as soul of the world. Even in relation to the natural world only, they have emerged as of limited value. If they are proposed for wider use as expressive of God's creative relationship to the world as a whole, our attitude towards them needs to be far more critical. Here, too, despite the *prima facie* contrast between the two pictures, the objection to both is essentially the same. Neither allows for the measure of human freedom that I have argued is essential to any satisfactory doctrine of creation. The shortcomings of the model of the potter and the clay are clear from scripture itself. Paul is misled by it into a disastrous attempt to stifle the human sense of moral outrage at the apparent injustices in the ordering of the world. 'Who are you, a man, to answer back to God? Can the pot speak to the potter and say "Why did you make me like this?" Surely the potter can do what he likes with the clay' (Rom. 9.20–21). Commentators, ancient and modern, have been left to make what they can of such a sentiment within the sacred text.[16] But the other picture of God as the soul of the world is clearly no better. Whatever value it may have for depicting God's relation to the inanimate order, it leaves no room at all for human freedom. And even if human consciousness and human action could in some way be accommodated within such a picture we would have to acknowledge that the self who is claimed to find expression through them could not (even allowing for some unresponsiveness or malfunctioning of the body) be the God of Christian faith. Too much sin and evil would come within those things that the model requires us to see as forms of God's self-expression.

Is there then any other model open to us, which will leave more room for the independence on which I have been insisting? Austin Farrer suggests at one point the model of 'the good novelist who . . . gets a satisfactory story out of the natural behaviour of the characters he conceives'.[17] Dorothy Sayers regarded that as the best available analogy to creation out of nothing.[18] She claims that 'the free-will of a genuinely created character has a certain reality, which the author will deny at his peril'.[19] But she is properly cautious about this claimed independence of characters within the novel. It is certainly something very much less substantial than the independence of real people. The model may be strengthened a little if we move from the idea of a novel to that of an improvised drama, in which the actors are each given the basic character of the person he or she is to represent and the general setting in which their interaction is to be worked out but in which they are left free to determine experimentally how the drama is to develop. In the process of getting deeper into their parts and discovering their reactions to one another in the given situation, they may be led on to enact the kind of drama which the author had always intended and already envisaged in principle though not in detail. The resultant drama would be both the author's and the actors', though we would be more ready to speak of the author as agent of the drama as a whole than as agent of any of the individual speeches or incidents within it.

All such analogies are inadequate to their task and this one is no exception. But there are differing degrees of inadequacy, and the older better established pictures do much less justice to the necessary concept of human freedom. Whatever the limitation of my own suggested picture, it will have served a useful purpose if it helps to oust some of the other, seriously misleading pictures that we have inherited from the past. For the moment I put it forward as a working model, to be further tested as we move on to consider the problems of evil and of providence.

4

Whence Comes Evil?

The problem of evil kept Augustine away from Christian faith for a decade.[1] It has kept many more from that faith for much longer, both before and since. It is the Achilles' heel of a rational Christian theism. The atrocities of the twentieth century have intensified the problem, psychologically if not theoretically. Is it possible, it is asked, to do theology after Auschwitz and Hiroshima? And if it is, must not that theology eschew the task of theodicy altogether? The attempt to make sense of evil in God's world, it is suggested, is an impossibility, and the attempt leads not only to failure but to blasphemy.

This proposal for the abandonment of theodicy is a tempting one. There is certainly no chapter in this book I would have been happier to persuade myself I was justified in omitting than this one. Moreover the argument can, and does, make strong appeal to the primary treatment of the subject within scripture, the Book of Job. Does not the form of God's answer to Job out of the whirlwind teach us that suffering is not a problem to be solved, but a mystery to be accepted in an existential awareness of the incomparability of God's being?[2] May it not be claimed that the Judaeo-Christian tradition of belief has been truest to itself when it has 'adopted Job's stance of accepting what it cannot understand' and that 'anything less . . . misses the reality of tragedy and the deep-down demonic that runs through this world's history'?[3] Paul Ricoeur puts the challenge in its sharpest form when, once again in reflection on the Book of Job, he speaks of 'the death of the God of providence'[4] and declares bluntly that 'the path of theodicy has here been closed off'.[5] But the appeal, for all its practical and religious attractiveness, has to be resisted, unless we are prepared to accept a wholly fideistic grounding of our faith. We cannot renounce all attempts at theodicy in principle without renouncing the use of critical reason in relation to faith altogether. And then we would be left without any check on the claims made by the person of faith, however fantastic. Much as we might like to be relieved of the obligation of theodicy, the attempt has still to be made. Indeed the philosophers, who with one breath tell us to abandon the task, do not entirely abandon it themselves. If by 'the death of the God of providence' Ricoeur means the impossibility of believing in a God who is directly involved in the determination of everything that happens in the world, then his protest is fully justified. But that does not in itself spell the end of all theodicy. Indeed, when Ricoeur goes on to suggest that the prophet, if not the philosopher, may perhaps speak of another 'God who would not protect me but would surrender me to the dangers of a life worthy of being called human' and adds the further comment 'Is not this God the crucified one?', we are hearing the theodicist within him still struggling to stay alive.[6] Charles Hartshorne, a philosopher of a very different hue, makes the more positive claim that the Book of Job redirects rather than rules out the task of theodicy; what Job learns when God addresses him out of the whirlwind is not, according to Hartshorne, that he has been presumptuous 'in daring, weak as he is, to challenge the divine majesty, but rather in daring, limited in experience as he is, to suppose that he knows what one means in saying God "does" such and such'.[7]

It is precisely the issues which Ricoeur and Hartshorne emphasize that are at the heart of our concern: a sense of God who is not the absolute controller and a new understanding of what it means to talk of God acting. So if the task of theodicy has still, however reluctantly, to be undertaken, there are hints that the lines of thought I am trying to follow out in this book may be the lines along which it ought to proceed. But such hints must not lead us to forget the salutary note of warning. Our attempt may well fail. But it may fail in a stronger or a weaker sense. Reflection on the horror and apparent pointlessness of so much evil in the world may lead to an abandonment of theistic belief. But it may also be the case that, while we have to acknowledge the fact of evil as in itself pointing away from faith in God, it does not do so in a manner that outweighs other aspects of our experience that point towards such a faith. There is no clear-cut procedure for 'weighing' such disparate forms of evidence, but it is a kind of judging that we do frequently have to practise. We may reasonably judge someone to be trustworthy, even though there are features of his or her observed behaviour that seem to weigh against that judgment and we have no other explanation of that particular behaviour that we are able to offer.[8] We do not have to produce a final solution of the problem of evil for it to be proper for us to maintain faith in God, even God the absolute creator. But we do need to go on struggling with the problem, if that faith is not to abandon its credentials to be a reasonable faith.

Augustine ultimately found his answer to the problem in the fall of Adam and the doctrine of original sin. For the story of Adam to fulfil that role it had to be developed in a way which would bring out the total responsibility of Adam for his sin. To that end it was essential to stress the absolute perfection of the original creation. Traditional accounts of a golden age in the past were truer than they knew. That original perfection appertained not only to the physical world, the garden within which human life was set; it applied to the nature of the original man and woman also. They were not only of incomparable beauty and immune to all physical ills; more importantly their intellectual powers surpassed those of even the greatest of their descendants to the degree that the flight of the bird surpasses the motion of the tortoise.[9] This aspect of the tradition – and its long endurance – is entertainingly illustrated by some words of Bishop Bull as late as the end of the seventeenth century, when he describes the ability of Adam, faced with an infinite variety of creatures he has never seen before:

. . . on a sudden, without study or premeditation, to give names to each of them so adapted and fitted to their natures as that God himself should approve the nomenclature. How astonishing a thing is it: what single man among all the philosophers since the Fall, what Plato, what Aristotle among the ancients, what Descartes or Gassendi among the moderns, nay, what Royal Society durst have undertaken this?[10]

Nor was this a matter of intellectual excellence only in any narrow sense of the word 'intellect'. As originally created man was perfectly attuned to God, and nothing stood in the way of his continuance in that condition – nothing, that is, except his own choice. The picture was designed to bring out the unqualified goodness of God's creation and the equally unqualified responsibility of Adam for every aspect of evil which is now endemic to it.

For Adam's wickedness was not only an evil in itself. It had evil consequences that infected every aspect of human life. Natural evils, in so far as such a concept was allowed at all, could be presented as derivative from human wickedness. It was a consequence of Adam's sin that men had to earn their livelihood by the sweat of their brow and women to suffer pain in childbirth. But it was not only such external evils that were to be traced back to Adam's sin. That sin had its repercussions in the inner life of human beings themselves. Reason was no longer capable of controlling the choices and actions of men and women. The distorting influence of the passions was now too strong. Sexual intercourse, originally intended simply for the procreation of children, had become inseparable from over-mastering passions which blinded men and women to the recognition of their highest good. And what was true of sexual passion was true of every facet of human experience. Men and women were no longer able to discern and choose the good consistently. The argument, if valid, is impressively comprehensive in its engagement with the problem. It leads to the conclusion that there is no form of evil that needs to be laid at

God's door. Yet it is not without difficulties even on its own terms. Does it make sense to speak of so perfect a creation, however free, in so perfect a setting, deliberately choosing to turn away from the good which it so fully enjoys? Augustine himself acknowledges the problem but argues that the question is unanswerable in principle.[11] In the light of that admission, might we not do better in the end to describe the purported explanation as a vivid account of the inexplicability of evil?

But that question is not one that we need to pursue. Because for us the story is not even a possible candidate for the explanatory role it has played in the past. To fulfil that role the historicity of the story is essential. The earliest Christians were fully aware of the symbolic character of the narrative. But symbolism was not incompatible with historicity. And historicity in this case could not be sacrificed to the allegorizers without undermining the explanatory power of the story, as an Eastern contemporary of Augustine's so perceptively points out. Theodore of Mopsuestia challenges the allegorizers in these terms:

> Their wish is to deny any difference between the whole of the history recorded in divine Scripture and dreams that occur at night. Adam, they say, is not Adam – this being a place where they are especially prone to interpret divine Scripture in a spiritual way (spiritual interpretation is what they like to have their nonsense called) – paradise is not paradise and the serpent is not a serpent. What I would like to say in reply to them is that once they start removing bits of history they will be left without any history at all. In that case, they must tell us how they will be in a position to say who was the first man to be created or how man became disobedient or how the sentence of death was introduced.[12]

We who cannot avoid acknowledging the unhistorical character of the narrative have to accept what Theodore was so unwilling to accept. The narrative cannot tell us how man became disobedient. Whatever continuing value the story may have, it cannot function for us as an explanation of evil which frees God of responsibility for its presence in the world. Any modern equivalent of the doctrine of original sin needs to modify the name as well as the substance of the doctrine. For it must be content to concern itself with the phenomenology and not with the genesis of evil. Its role has to be seen as descriptive rather than explanatory. Its classic expression in scripture will be better found in Paul's analysis of his inability to do the good that he would in chapter 7 of the Epistle to the Romans than in his account of sin's entry into the world through one man in chapter 5. The doctrine, in other words, acknowledges that human life and its environment are radically disordered within our experience however far back we trace it. It acknowledges that fact as in *prima facie* conflict with the doctrine of creation, but affirms that it does not overwhelm it.

Two twentieth-century theologians have given particularly forceful expression to this way of taking over the old tradition. Paul Tillich insists on the presence of a tragic element, as well as a moral element, in evil. He even speaks of 'a coincidence of creation and Fall', but claims that it is not a logical coincidence and therefore does not make sin a 'rational necessity'.[13] And Paul Ricoeur sums up the significance of the story of the Fall in this way:

> By the myth anthropology is invited, in the first place, to gather all the sins of the world into a sort of transhistorical unity, symbolized by the first man; then to put the stamp of contingency on that radical evil; and finally to preserve, superimposed on one another, the goodness of created man and the wickedness of historical man, while 'separating' the one from the other by the 'event' which the myth tells of as the first sin of the first man . . . Man is 'destined' for the good and 'inclined' to evil; in this paradox of 'destination' and 'inclination' the whole meaning of the symbol of the fall is concentrated.[14]

Whether the 'paradox' rules out all further rational reflection and closes off the path of theodicy entirely as the earlier citation from Ricoeur asserts, we must judge when we have assayed that path. For to that path we are committed. Ricoeur's words should not hold us back from the attempt, though they are an important reminder of its hazardous nature.

Once we have rejected, as we have, the escape-hatch of a radical dualism, we are committed to accepting some form of positive relation, however indirect, between evil and God's will. Even process theology, despite its abandonment of creation *ex nihilo*, has found it necessary to speak of God as 'responsible for evil though not indictable for it'.[15] Evil was part of the risk taken by God in bringing a world into being out of the triviality of the pre-existing chaos. A similar line of reflection is not ruled out for the upholder of creation *ex nihilo*. God's good purpose in creation, it may be argued, cannot be achieved without allowing for the emergence of evil. If that 'cannot' could be shown to be an ontologically necessary 'cannot', then the position would be essentially the same as for the process theologian. For then the argument in both cases would be not whether God might not have created a world free from evil, but whether God should or should not have created a world at all. But we can hardly expect to pursue an argument of that degree of generality to the point at which an ontologically necessary connection could be demonstrated between the emergence of evil and the purpose of creation. The most we can hope to do is to reflect as carefully as we can on the nature of such connections as we believe ourselves able to discern between the two. Those reflections need to be pursued along two related, but distinguishable, lines. We might call them internal and external relations; they correspond more or less to the traditional distinction between sin and natural evil. Despite their close interrelation neither can be subsumed under the other. Some evil actions may, for example, be due entirely to brain damage or chemical deficiency; but not all fall within such categories unless we are prepared to take the drastic and unjustifiable step of denying the validity of the concept of moral responsibility altogether. Similarly the disastrous character of some floods or famines may be exacerbated by the improvidence or greed of men and women; but that is not true of all natural disasters. We need to consider what sort of links there might be between both kinds of evil and the overall purpose of God in creation.

The argument at the internal level is one that is particularly well-traversed in philosophical debate, where it is known by the designation of the 'free-will defence'. On the one hand is the claim that the actuality, and not merely the possibility, of wrong choice is inherent in genuine freedom. Moral evil is seen as an indispensable ingredient in moral growth. On the other is the claim that there is no logical incoherence in the concept of God creating free beings who would always in practice freely choose the good.[16] Philosophically the arguments appear to me to be inconclusive. However little way along the desired path it may take us, it is important that the free-will defence should be at least a possible line of argument. If it could be shown conclusively that the idea of created beings who are from the start both wholly free and wholly good was a logically coherent conception, then this line of reflection would be effectively blocked off. Such a thesis would in the nature of things be very difficult to demonstrate, and I do not find the arguments for it convincing.

But however necessary, that line of argument is not sufficient even within the comparatively restricted range of the present discussion. We need to consider whether a similar line of argument can be applied also to the physical context in which our lives are set. Neither Tillich nor Ricoeur would wish to identify the picture they offer with the old Neo-platonic view that evil is implicit in limitation, so that a finite world free of evil is not strictly conceivable. Yet to speak of 'a coincidence of creation and Fall' points in that direction. Personal life requires a stable environment, with physical properties that do not alter to meet each person's changing needs. The degree of constancy that is necessary for ordered living, it may be argued, can hardly avoid being a source of disadvantage or damage to some people on some occasions. The difficulty of developing such an argument with any rigour is even greater than in the internal case. We have no other world with which to compare our own, and it is doubtful whether we can seriously conceive one. The most we can affirm is the possibility that personal life of the kind that we know is dependent on a physical environment which functions in fixed ways that cannot always be beneficent to every particular human need.

I have acknowledged the grave difficulty of assessing the validity of these suggested arguments. But the greatest difficulty about the position being adumbrated is the extent of evil in the world. Even if the arguments do have force, it is extremely hard to see how they could possibly explain the more massive evils, human and natural, of which we are aware. It is for this reason that many of the illustrations often appealed to in exposition of this line of reasoning seem dangerously to trivialize the issue. A headmaster, to take an example from a recent writing of Christopher Butler, may not be regarded as blameworthy for the bullying that takes place within his school, if that is felt to be an inevitable by-product of a system that contributes to the development of character.[17] But if the bullying went beyond a certain point, we would regard him as blameworthy unless prompt action were taken to bring it to an end. And does not our experience of Auschwitz and Hiroshima suggest that that point has long been passed? Langdon Gilkey makes the point tendentiously if effectively by describing Tennant's measured exposition of this line of argument as being 'extravagantly "English sportsman" ' and then going on to object:

> To us on the contrary it is as if these gentlemanly rugger players had suddenly produced knives and guns, so that at the end the field of life by no means rings with the happy shouts of tired athletes, but, rather, it is filled with the very real screams of mangled bodies and littered with very dead corpses.[18]

Gilkey is unfair to Tennant, since it is he and not Tennant who introduces the language of the sportsfield. But it does give forceful expression to a valid point. In terms of the image of an improvised drama that I put forward at the end of the last chapter, do we not have to acknowledge that the actors have decided to play the tragedy for real, in a way that can hardly correspond to the author's original intention? As a direction for thought about why a world might not be free of all evil, this line of reflection seems promising; but as an adequate explanation accounting for the whole volume of evil it falls a long way short of what we seem to require.

So far we have been considering evil in relation to the doctrine of creation. Traditionally it has had closer links with the doctrine of redemption. One characteristic of the general approach I have adopted is a tendency to reduce the distance between those two doctrines. A theology which can speak of 'a coincidence of creation and Fall' will be well advised to speak also in terms of a coincidence of creation, fall and redemption. If evil is somehow inherent in the creative process, so too must be the overcoming of that evil. Two sayings from St John's Gospel serve to provide traditional support for such an emphasis. In John 5.17 Jesus responds to the accusation that he has healed the paralytic on the sabbath with the words: 'My Father works hitherto, and I work.' His healing work is all one with God's creative work. And in John 9.3 Jesus rejects the suggestion that the affliction of the man born blind is a punishment for sin: 'It is not that this man sinned or his parents, but that the glory of God might be manifested in him.' The misfortunes of life are part of the context of our lives and are not individually directed, either as punishment or (as a superficial reading of the text might suggest) for God to win glory from the situation. The significance of the man's blindness is not to be sought in relation to its origins; at that level it is simply a part of the accidentality of life. It is to be sought in relation to its overcoming. And that process of the overcoming of evil, though conceptually distinguishable from creation, is an integral part of the gradual emergence of God's world. In John Hick's terms God's one action is his continuous creation/salvation of the world.[19] The theme of the overcoming of evil, or in traditional language the idea of redemption, offers a second context for reflection on evil in relation to the activity of God.

Traditional teaching about redemption finds its primary

expression in terms of specific acts of God in human history. In that respect it will fall within the discussion of providence to which we shall be coming in the next chapter. For the moment we are concerned rather with what we may call the background conditions of redemption; and the underlying issue is how we may conceive God's relation to the world's experience of evil. One important aspect of the doctrines of the incarnation and the cross has been to stress the voluntary and intimate character of God's involvement in the consequences of evil. The tradition, even while insisting on the full divinity of the crucified, has often been hesitant to draw out the natural conclusions of that conviction in terms of God's relation to suffering. The doctrine of divine impassibility did not rule out the idea altogether; it could hardly do so for a faith which affirms that the most fundamental characteristic of God is love. Yet it did qualify the notion in ways which often resulted in a weakening of its force. But I have already argued for a doctrine of creation which can at the same time safeguard the important truth contained in the doctrine of divine impassibility and also remove the inhibitions so often felt about a full expression of God's involvement in the suffering of the world.[20] If God is 'responsible' for evil, in however modified a sense, because he has taken the risk of creating a world in which it was highly likely, or even logically bound, to emerge, then there are strong moral objections to any view of God which regards him as immune from the damaging consequences of that evil. The picture that we have drawn of the relation between God as creator and the evil in the world makes it incumbent on us to be able also to say of God, in the haunting words of scripture, that 'in all their afflictions, he was afflicted' (Isa. 63.9). We cannot claim the authority of the ancient prophet for that sentiment, for the words are in fact a mistranslation. But the idea is implicit in the general picture of God's compassion to be found in so much of both Old and New Testaments, as well as being a requisite element within any moral theism.

We have claimed to meet the rightful concerns of the doctrine of impassibility by insisting that God's involvement in the suffering of the world does not mean that he is the victim of a situation that is simply imposed on him from outside. The evil may be of purely human devising; but the conditions that have made such devising possible derive from God. But it is not enough to show that God, though victim, is not absolute victim. Christian theology needs also to depict God as at the same time victor in and through his involvement in the world's evil. One way in which that need has traditionally been met is by a doctrine of redemption which is centred not simply on the cross, but on the cross and resurrection understood as a composite unity. The resurrection in such an understanding is seen not simply as a reversal of the cross, but as its final fulfilment; there is symbolic significance in the depiction of the risen Christ as 'the lamb with the marks of slaughter upon him' (Rev. 5.6). Once again our concern at this point is not with cross and resurrection in their historical enactment (to that we shall come later), but with the idea of God's relation to evil implicit in such a doctrine of redemption. God's sharing in the consequences of the world's evil may be a morally necessary condition of Christian faith, but it is not sufficient for a Christian doctrine of redemption. We need to affirm more of God than his involvement in the tragedies of finite existence; it is not enough simply to describe him as 'the fellow-sufferer who understands'. Process theology, with its denial of God's absolute control and its strong sense of human freedom, has found it necessary to affirm the absoluteness of the risk taken by God in creating a world; there is no scope within a scheme for which process is fundamental for any conception of an ultimate fulfilment of purposes for which that risk was undertaken. In that respect process theology would seem to exacerbate rather than to alleviate the problem of evil; in such a context the concept of God's 'responsibility' for evil seems even harder to accept. I have argued earlier that the strong sense of human freedom and creativity which process theology is determined to maintain can be affirmed within a theology that continues to affirm the absoluteness of God's creative work. May it perhaps also be compatible with a continued insistence that the intention of that creative work will not finally be thwarted? The religious sense of God as final succour believes that it is. It does not deny the risk inherent in creation. But it sees it as a risk of disasters on the road (a risk that would appear to have been abundantly realized) rather than a risk of ultimate failure.

Is such a conviction justifiable? Certainly we must not speak as if human life was without significant fulfilments in the present. There is much in the experience of beauty and of love that leads us to speak of the world as good and to prompt a sense of gratitude for the fact of existence. And that sense can in practice continue to coexist with considerable personal experience of evil and suffering. But in the face of Auschwitz and Hiroshima, and of the countless other damaged and desperate lives that those names symbolize, it is not easy to see in those present fulfilments an adequate completion of God's purpose in creation. In the face of such evils, some future fulfilment of the more transcendent kind that has characterized traditional Christian faith seems also to be needed.

Two grave difficulties attend a contemporary affirmation of such a future hope. The first is that which has led to its abandonment by process theology. Can it be affirmed without reintroducing the idea of a divine control of human history in some ultimately unacceptable form? The difficulties are real but not, I believe, insuperable. It is the specificity of form and time-scale that has characterized so many of the prophecies of God's triumph that has made the whole notion appear incompatible with that radical independence and freedom with which, I have been arguing, God has endowed his creation. But God's purpose is fixed and unchanging only in the most general sense. God is affected by our actions in such a way that the particular form of that purpose is changed to take account of them. So if we affirm our confidence in God's ultimate triumph, we are not affirming that some fixed target will be reached, let alone that it will be reached by some predetermined date. It is a genuinely unknown future of which we are speaking. But we will be speaking out of our faith in the God who has taken the risk of creating the world, the unremitting character of whose love the Christian believes himself to have seen in the figure of

Christ, and on that basis expressing our confidence that the world will ultimately be expressive of God's will in a way which is not true now; that eventually we will be able to say, as we know we cannot say now, that what *is* is God's will. Our radical emphasis on human freedom may hold us back from claiming that this fulfilment of our confidence is a logically inescapable implicate of the risk that a God such as we have come to believe in has taken in creating a world. But we can argue that the work of that creation will not come to an end unless or until it is fulfilled. In the vivid words ascribed to Origen, 'Christ remains on the cross, as long as one sinner remains in hell'.[21]

The other difficulty is that of conceivability. In the light not only of what appears to occur at death but also of the deterioration of personality that we not infrequently see occurring before death, is it possible to claim that personal life as we now know it can find its fulfilment outside the physical finite world of our present experience? The most I believe that can be claimed is that our experience of ourselves as somehow transcending the components that constitute those selves makes the notion, however difficult, not philosophically absurd.[22] If there are grounds for affirming a moral theism, and if the fulfilment of personal life beyond our present order of existence is a necessary feature of that moral theism, it can still be responsibly affirmed.

But our present concern is with an attempt to understand the place of evil in God's world. And in that context the final emphasis needs to be placed elsewhere. Even if the difficulties concerning a final fulfilment of God's purposes could be fully dispersed (and I acknowledge that the arguments I have adumbrated fall far short of that), our attempted theodicy would still be incomplete. Even the fullest and most universal hope for the future of humankind could not be claimed as satisfying our protests at the sheer brutality of some of the forms of suffering and evil with which the world is beset. Ivan Karamazov's challenge would still stand and Alyosha's response be the right one for us to make:

'Imagine that you are creating a fabric of human destiny with the object of making men happy in the end, giving them peace and rest at last, but that it was essential and inevitable to torture to death only one tiny creature – that baby beating its breast with its fist, for instance – and to found that edifice on its unavenged tears, would you consent to be the architect on those conditions? Tell me, and tell the truth.'

'No, I wouldn't consent,' said Alyosha softly.[23]

In that sense our theodicy fails, as Ricoeur warned us it would. Faith in God remains faith in God maintained in spite of the opposing evidence of evil. If our attempted theodicy has been of any value, it has been in putting forward a framework from within which the contradiction of evil, though not dissolved, appears less absolute than in some others. Although we must continue to walk by faith and not by sight, this perspective may enable us to claim, hesitantly but honestly, that that faith is not a wholly blind and unreasonable faith.

There was no one place at which it was clearly most appropriate to introduce this consideration of evil within the course of the argument that I am trying to develop. For it is the dark shadow that sharpens both the point and the difficulty of every theological affirmation. To start with it would have been to raise it without an appropriate context for discussion. To end with it would have been to treat it as an appendix, which did not need to be raised until everything else had been settled. The place that I have chosen for it, at the mid-point of my discussion, is intended as a symbol of its inescapability for Christian reflection. But raising it at this point, before we have moved on to the more historical side of the discussion, has led to a concentration on the more formal aspects of the issues involved. But the problem will remain with us as we move on to questions of providence, christology and grace, and it will have its contribution to make towards the determination of what can and cannot properly be affirmed there. Moreover, that further discussion may also in its turn have a contribution to make towards any assessment of the validity of the lines of reflection outlined in this chapter.

5

Providence and Public History

The suggestion I have offered so far is that we should see the gradual emergence of our world as a single divine act. In other words it is a purposeful occurrence, whose disparate features are held together by a unity of intention. We cannot claim to grasp that purpose fully, but we need to be able to give some indication of its nature. We may perhaps speak of it provisionally as maximizing the growth of personal freedom and creativity within relationships of love both at the human level and between human beings and God.

The starting point for any discussion of providence must be the affirmation that such a purpose is in some measure reflected in the world as we know it. However important eschatology may be for faith, the Christian God is no *deus ex machina* who comes in at the end and simply reverses the direction in which everything had been moving up to that point. Thus John Macquarrie writes of creativity as 'an ordered movement into ever fuller and richer kinds of being' and goes on: 'Faith in providence asserts this definite movement in the creation, an overcoming of deficiencies and distortions and a fuller realizing of potentialities.'[1] If that were all there were to be said, the doctrine of providence would take on the same purely phenomenological character that I have argued is appropriate with relation to the doctrine of original sin.[2] Providence would simply be a name for that overall creativity or tendency towards growth and development which is characteristic of the way the world goes. But theologians are less willing to spell out the doctrine exclusively in such terms in the case of providence than they are in the case of original sin. Macquarrie goes on to express doubts about the adequacy of his initial statement. He wants to be able to distinguish providence from fate or from 'a self-righting mechanism'. He expresses himself anxious to do more justice to the kind of understanding of providence reflected in the biblical story. The possibility of doing precisely that is at the heart of our enquiry too. How Macquarrie sees himself able to do it is therefore of particular interest. What he proposes is offered only as a tentative analogy; it is 'the analogy of a strong chess player who, whatever move his opponent will make, can still bring the game around to the way he intends it to go'.[3] John Lucas suggests a similar analogy in response to the same problem. His is the picture of Persian rugmakers, where father and children work simultaneously at the two ends of the rug; whatever mistakes the inexperienced children may make at their end, the experienced father is able to incorporate them within a continually revised but wholly satisfying pattern by the weaving he himself does at the other end of the rug.[4] These analogies are instructive. In rejecting the more general, mechanical account that fails to do justice to traditional teaching, they offer an alternative which certainly does not (as some accounts do) ride roughshod over the reality of human freedom. The analogies depict God's actions as clearly distinguishable from the actions of at least some human agents. But that leaves the nature and location of God's action highly problematic. How and where does God make his moves in the game of chess? Which are the threads that are of his weaving? These questions remain, and are not easy to answer.

Do we need to answer them? Is it incumbent on us, if we are to go on affirming a traditional view of providence along the lines that Macquarrie proposes, to be able to indicate how and where God's moves are being made? There is certainly no difficulty in general principle with the idea of there being both a theological and a physical account of the emergence of the world. We have noted earlier how we can give two accounts of the same happening (a car swerving off the road and going over a cliff), one in terms of the observed physical phenomena and the other in terms of an intended human action.[5] Similarly we are well used to the idea of different scientific disciplines each giving its own account of the same occurrence. We might, for example, want to describe a breakdown in the functioning of a human body in biochemical and in psychological terms. Where we do have difficulty in such cases is in our attempts to describe how those different accounts are related to one another. It is a difficulty of that kind that we cannot avoid in our present discussion. For the doctrine of providence has been understood to involve more than a general relation of the world as a whole to a divine purpose. It has spoken of God determining the way the world goes at particular points in its emergence and more emphatically at particular points in human history. God makes specific moves in the chess-game of life. It is the intelligibility of that concept, one which will not allow the theological account to float free of the physical and historical accounts, that we are seeking to probe.

How is such an enquiry to be conducted? It is important not to set out on the task with unreasonable expectations of what is needed to justify the affirmation of God's providential activity. We are not looking for a divine causation that can be neatly fitted in as a missing factor within our existing historical or physical accounts; that would be to treat God as just one more causal agent alongside others in the world. Nor should we expect God's activity to be directly or immediately observable; ancient tradition and modern sensitivity alike have stressed the hidden nature of God's providence. But if it is altogether hidden, how can we justify our affirmation of it? Here two contrasting strategies seem to be open to us.

Charles Wood tackles the issue in a recent article with the help of categories we have already employed. He asks how at the human level we distinguish between 'act' and 'accident' or mere 'occurrence'. We do so, he argues, either by inference or by the agent's own account. Either the driver of the car which swerved off the road tells us what happened, if he or she survives to tell the tale, or the road accident investigator has to infer which it was on the basis of his or her experience of similar cases in the past. But, Wood argues, divine agency is so unique in character that the way of inference is closed off for us. The only way of identifying God's acts is the way of the agent's self-disclosure. It is only through the Word of God that the identification and interpretation of God's acts is made possible for us. But, as Wood readily and rightly acknowledges, God's Word 'is also hidden to the undiscerning eye or ear'. It is therefore hard to see how it can fulfil the role ascribed to it. 'God's Word,' and I quote Wood again, 'is God's act.'[6] It too, therefore, needs to be identified and interpreted. So we appear to have embarked upon an infinite regress, unless at some point we can tread the path of inference. It is that path, therefore, that I shall try to pursue.

A useful account of how this second strategy may be pursued is given in another recent article by David Galilee and Brian Hebblethwaite. In a description of Austin Farrer's work they write as follows:

> The divine Spirit 'radiates' upon his creation, superimposing higher levels of organization and drawing the various threads of evolution, history and individual life-stories into the providential patterns we observe. The modality of the divine Spirit's operation may be unknown, the hand of God perfectly hidden, but the effects of the divine agency in the emergence of man, in salvation-history, and in the lives of Christ and the saints are not hidden at all. Moreover they are particular effects requiring us to postulate particular action, even if that action is mediated through the whole field of creaturely interaction. Once again the clearest example is the experience of grace, where a man's conversion, forgiveness, inspiration or enlightenment must be represented as an act of God, however mediated by secondary causes.[7]

That passage claims that the emergence of man, salvation-history and the lives of Christ and of the saints are not merely consistent with but require us to affirm particular acts of God in history. I have already questioned that judgment in relation to the emergence of the human race. I argued earlier that while it may very well lead us to affirm the whole process of creation as God's act, it does not by itself require us to speak of particular divine actions within that process.[8] The life of Christ and the experience of grace, which Galilee and Hebblethwaite regard as the most compelling evidence, will concern us in subsequent chapters. It is the intermediate area of so-called 'salvation-history' that I want to consider in the remainder of this chapter.

The idea of history as under the providential direction of God has always been, as we saw much earlier, a distinctive feature of both Judaism and Christianity.[9] The sense of themselves as a specially chosen people was at the heart of Jewish religious faith. The story of the Exodus, which was seen as the originating and paradigmatic experience of that national faith, depicts God as calling the people of Israel out of Egypt, so that they could serve him in a promised land. But it was not a faith that was easily established or maintained. It was tried and refined in the fires of national adversity. The fall of Jerusalem might have seemed to negate any claim of God's providential care of Israel. It could well have been taken to imply that God had abandoned and repudiated his people. But the prophets came to see it as an act of judgment, falling within a credible interpretation of providence. The Assyrian conqueror was 'the rod of God's anger' (Isa. 10.5). And Jeremiah was able to go further and see it also in more positive terms as freeing the way for a less narrowly based and more deeply personal form of faith in the new covenant of the future. So too the Christian church refused to see the crucifixion as implying God's repudiation of Jesus, but came to interpret it as fully consonant with God's providential concern for the salvation of humankind.

As Christianity developed its own specific understanding of God's providence, the primary emphasis was on a vision of history as leading up to the coming of Christ. The idea of a convergence of history on to the figure of Christ took a variety of forms. Its most obvious form was Christ as the fulfilment of prophecy. The concept of prophecy was not restricted to the foretelling of particular occurrences. Though it certainly included that, it also embraced various forms of typology, whereby the pattern of earlier lives and of past events was seen as foreshadowing the pattern of Christ's life, and especially his death and resurrection. Nor was the idea of God's providential preparation for the coming of Christ confined to its Jewish antecedents. As Eusebius, the first church historian, looked back three hundred years later on that originating event of Christian faith, he envisaged an even wider panorama of God's providential care. He expressed it in these words:

> No one who reflects upon the matter can fail to be convinced that it was no mere human accident that the majority of the nations of the world never came under the unifying rule of Rome until the time of Jesus. For his wonderful visitation of humankind coincided with Rome's attainment of the acme of power . . . And no one can deny that it was not without God's help that this should have happened at the very same time that the teaching about our Saviour took its rise. Consider the difficulties involved in the disciples' journeying, had the nations been under separate governments and therefore not having any dealings with one another. But with those separate governments abolished, the disciples could accomplish their projects in safety. The supreme God had smoothed the way before them, controlling the animosities of those hostile to true religion through fear of a strong central government.[10]

Nor indeed did that providence cease with the coming of Christ. As one who had been an active participant in the process of the transformation of the Roman empire from persecutor to upholder of the church, Eusebius could hardly help but see the continuation of God's hand at work there. He describes the great events of his own lifetime in these terms:

> Then the divine and heavenly grace showed how favourably and propitiously it watched over us, and even our rulers, the very people who had been waging war against us for so long,

changed their attitude in the most remarkable way. They issued a recantation and, with merciful edicts and humane ordinances, they quenched the fire of persecution that had blazed so furiously against us. But this was not due to any human agency; it was not a result of anything that could be described as pity or humanity on the part of the rulers . . . It was divine providence itself, which became reconciled to the church and at the same time attacked the perpetrator of these evils . . . A divinely-sent punishment, I say, executed vengeance upon him beginning with his flesh and going on to the soul.[11] (I will spare my readers, as Eusebius does not spare his, the grisly details of Galerius' fatal illness.)

One could hardly imagine a more comprehensive affirmation of the providentially directed character of human history than that. And something along those lines has remained throughout human history as the underlying assumption, the basic framework within which all particular Christian doctrines have been seen and understood. Most Christians today would be reluctant to express themselves in the same confident and detailed way that Eusebius does, but the strongly historical character of Christian faith holds them back from abandoning his general picture altogether. But how are we to envisage so vast and complex a direction of what happens in the world being exercised? Can we continue today to affirm some such version of the Christian story, without having to re-introduce an unacceptable notion of God the absolute controller?

In trying to answer these questions I want to look in turn at three aspects of such an account of the providential guidance of history. Many of the events through which God's providential activity is understood to have been carried out were done through the agency of pagan empires and emperors. What I want to consider first, therefore, is the vital role apparently played by human agents with no awareness of any kind that they might be fulfilling a role in the purposes of God. Austin Farrer argued strongly for the intelligibility of the conception of what he called 'double agency', even in those cases where the intended meanings of the two agents, divine and human, were utterly different from one another. But he acknowledged that no account of the connection between the two was possible, because of our ignorance of 'the modality of the divine action'.[12] John Lucas has recently been credited by Vincent Brümmer with offering an analysis which is a 'distinct advance' on Farrer's, precisely on the grounds that 'Farrer fails to provide an explanation of exactly how, on his theory, God's agency is related to that of man'.[13] The example that Brümmer quotes from Lucas as an illustration of this improved account is the building of Solomon's temple. We can perfectly well say that Solomon built the temple and that his stonemason built it.[14] This is indeed a clear illustration of the fact that there is no difficulty in principle in ascribing a single event to two agents. Nor is such a way of speaking invalidated by the fact that they may have had very different motives for what they did. Solomon may have built the temple to God's glory (or his own); the stonemason may have built it to earn a living or to escape the unpleasant consequences of evading the draft. But the analogy does not help us in our search for an intelligible account of how we can properly speak of God acting providentially through the varied activities of Assyrian, Persian and Roman emperors and warlords. Nor indeed does Lucas ever suggest that it could fulfil that particular role. We can only use the language we do in the case of Solomon and the stonemason because there is an evident link between the two. Solomon issues an edict and the stonemason acts, whether willingly or reluctantly, because of it. It is the absence of any parallel to that element in the analogy that must give us pause before we accept it too readily as meeting our difficulty. Let us take the example of Cyrus. He is spoken of by the prophet as God's shepherd to carry out all God's purpose for Israel, although (as the prophet explicitly declares) he does not know God (Isa. 44.28; 45.4). So the restoration of Israel after the exile is both Cyrus' doing and God's doing. Cyrus' political ambitions lead him to bring about certain results that coincide with God's will for his people. But that by itself does not justify us in speaking of it as a particular action of God in human history. To do that, we would need to be able to specify at least what kind of link there might be between the two, between the divine intention and the bringing about of the result. And with a Cyrus who does not know God and is bent on military conquest, it is difficult to see even in the most formal terms what kind of link there could be – unless it were some hidden manipulation of Cyrus' deliberative processes. But that leads us back to the all-controlling God who does not respect the freedom of the world he has created. And that God we have already seen good reason to repudiate. So too does John Lucas. That is made clear when he does consider a case comparable to those with which we are concerned. He discusses Hitler's 'providential' holding back of his panzers at the time of Dunkirk, and comments as follows:

> God's influence is to be seen not in an arbitrary interference with Hitler's free-will, but in having made men as he has made them, with the grain of human nature such that God's purposes tend to be fulfilled, and that those who would frustrate them are frustrated.[15]

Reflection on what is involved in cases of this kind, which are so integral to the traditional understanding of God's providential direction of history, inescapably leads us back to general statements about the kind of world God has created rather than to claims about particular, specifiable acts of God in history.

The second feature of the providential account of Christian history which I want to consider, is its understanding of the coming of Christ as the fulfilment of prophecy. In the New Testament this prophetic fulfilment is often affirmed in a highly specific form. The soldiers involved in the crucifixion of Jesus cast lots for his tunic instead of tearing it because that was what the Psalmist had foretold (John 19.23–24; Ps. 22.18), and one of them pierced his side with a lance because a piercing had been predicted by Zechariah (John 19.34–37; Zech. 13.10). There has been much debate as to whether prediction of this sort, grounded in a belief in the omniscience of God, is or is not consistent with human freedom. The Boethian defence of omniscience as not strictly foreknowledge but rather a timeless knowing, even if valid in other contexts, will not help us here. For *pred*iction implies *fore*knowledge, and that is logically incompatible with the understanding of creation for which I have argued. The point is well made by Brian Hebblethwaite, who writes:

> God has so made the world, with its temporal structure and open future, that the task of constructing a specific future has been given to the creature. God's omniscience, like his omnipotence, is self-limited by the nature of what he has made. In each case the limitation is logical, given the actual nature of God's creation. He cannot determine the future without destroying his creatures' freedom. He cannot know the future precisely, if his creatures are indeed free.[16]

Certainly the sort of fulfilment of prediction implied by the scriptural texts cited seems inconceivable apart from a manipulative control of human action that is wholly unacceptable. But it is not only difficult to conceive; it would in any case be religiously trivial. There is a predictive element within the Old Testament tradition, but it is not the heart or substance of Old Testament prophecy. Moreover, it has been claimed that even the New Testament writers did not intend their words to be taken so literally, but saw the instances they quoted not so much as individual fulfilments of significance in themselves, but rather as pointers to a wider pattern of fulfilment.[17] The case is overstated, but certainly a highly specific form of prediction was never central to a seriously argued Christian case. The early Christians had their own war to wage against fatalism and determinism. Moreover, however such links may have been originally intended, they very often came to be seen as primarily literary links of words or images helping us to grasp imaginatively broader similarities of a typological kind. Yet even when the main stress was laid on typological interpretations of that sort, they were not normally understood to exclude the predictive altogether. But whatever may or may not have been done in the past, there is certainly a strong case now for understanding them in that exclusive way. A revised understanding along such lines would open the way to a conception of the links between the life of Christ and the past, which would cut away the difficulties concerning God's action and human freedom implicit in the idea of prediction and at the same time make possible a religiously more profound appreciation of the historical process leading up to Christ.

Such a revised account would see the crucifixion as the archetypal example of a conflict between the purposes of God and the self-interest of men and women. Conflict of that kind had already been glimpsed and partially embodied at earlier points in history, but in Christ it is enacted in its purest form. For such an approach perhaps one of the best 'prophecies' of the crucifixion would be the words of the godless men in Wisdom 2.10–24, as they plot against the just man who 'styles himself the servant of the Lord' and 'is a living condemnation of all our ideas'. But it is wholly consonant also with more traditional 'prophetic' passages, such as Isaiah 53. A view of this kind is to be commended both for its compatibility with human freedom and for the quality of its religious insight. But it must be recognized that it involves no divine providence, in the sense of a specific divine foreseeing and overruling of events. The links between the life of Christ and what led up to it have rather the character of retrovidence – the seeing of significant patterns in anterior history after the event. Any prophetic foreseeing of the future can be accounted for by insight into human nature, giving rise by extrapolation to true vision of how things may be in the future. Understood in this way, no particular divine action is required to account for this aspect of the providential direction of history.

In traditional Christian teaching prophecy has frequently been twinned with miracle as the two primary pointers to that most important of all particular divine actions, the incarnation. However much accounts of the Christian story have emphasized God's working through the ordinary events of history, miracle has always had a part to play and it is to that theme that I wish now to turn. The early Christians did not find it difficult to offer a reasoned defence of the concept of miracle. Since creation itself, including the apparent regularities of nature, was entirely dependent on the will of God, there was nothing absurd in the idea that God might will things to happen in unaccustomed ways on some particular occasions. There was no ultimate conflict between the normal and abnormal occurrence, for both were equally dependent upon and expressive of the will of God. Even Aquinas for all his stress on secondary causation could allow that sometimes God, as primary cause, might act directly without any form of secondary causation, since secondary causes derive from God 'not out of a necessity of nature but by decision of his will'.[18] The conceivability of miracle continues to be the subject of much philosophical debate. Certainly the notion of miracle cannot simply be ruled out on scientific grounds as logically impossible, since the world we know is not a closed, deterministically ordered system. But that does not take us very far. There are many things that are not logically inconceivable, but that for all practical purposes we do regard as inconceivable. There is nothing logically inconceivable in the idea that every reader of this book may lay it down precisely at this point and read no further, but, if it is not complacent to say so, I do not, as I pen these words, regard it as a conceivable eventuality. So the conflict with the understanding of the world which underlies the work of both science and history, though not a logical conflict, is real and weighs heavily against acceptance of the possibility of miracle. But for the theist there is a counter-argument in support of the notion based on the human experience of personal agency. On the analogy of what are designated basic actions, it can be argued that 'just as a human agent does not violate natural law by deciding to raise his arm, so God does not violate natural law by deciding to move the wind in order to dry up the sea'.[19] Or, if one holds a contra-causal view of human freedom, it can be claimed that 'it would be rather surprising if God did not possess the same kind of freedom to act without causal restraint within the world'.[20] The more general question of the value and limitations of such arguments by analogy from persons in the

world to the transcendent God is something I shall be
discussing in the next chapter.[21] The aim of this particular
analogy is to take the theist, before he studies the evidence for
or against particular miracles, beyond the point of accepting
their conceivability and encourage him to regard them as
probable. But there are obvious and important differences
between the human and the divine cases. However difficult it
may be to give an account of human action, and of the relation
between the human mind and the physical causal system that it
appears to entail, it is something of which we have straightforward and immediate experience. In the case of the purported
direct divine actions that we call miracles, the evidence for most
of us at least is much less direct or inescapable. That difference
seems to me sufficiently great to make the argument less than
compelling.

But whatever the outcome of such philosophical debate, the
concept has also to face serious religious difficulties.[22] If the
direct action of God, independent of secondary causation, is an
intelligible concept, then it would appear to have been spar-
ingly and strangely used. Miracles must by definition be
relatively infrequent or else the whole idea of laws of nature,
even of a broadly statistical sort, would be undermined, and
ordered life as we know it an impossibility. Yet even so it would
seem strange that no miraculous intervention prevented Auschwitz or Hiroshima, while the purposes apparently forwarded
by some of the miracles acclaimed in traditional Christian faith
seem trivial by comparison. Thus to acknowledge even the
possibility of miracle raises acute problems for theodicy. But
can that possibility be denied? John Lucas says firmly that it
cannot. 'No theist,' he writes, 'would deny that God is
omnipotent, and that he could intervene to prevent any
particular event's occurring.'[23] It is perhaps somewhat rash to
assert what no theist would deny – unless the assertion be
regarded as one that is true by definition, in the sense that to
deny the possibility of miracle would render someone a deist
rather than a theist. But Brian Hebblethwaite, who is certainly
no deist, puts the point very differently. He does not deny the

conceivability of miracle on philosophical grounds, but the actuality of miracle is for him another matter. For the direct intervention of God, however rare the occasions of it, would in his view have disastrous implications for our understanding of the problem of evil.

> To suppose that he does so [i.e., God acts in the world by direct intervention] just occasionally would be to raise all the problems which perplex the believer as he reflects on the problem of evil, about why God does not intervene more often. It would also prevent him from appealing to the God-given structures of creation, and their necessary role in setting creatures at a distance from their creator and providing a stable environment for their lives, as an explanation for the physical ills which can afflict God's creatures.[24]

I have already argued that however incomplete that explanation may be, we cannot afford to do without it.[25] And since we have already allowed that 'God's . . . omnipotence is self-limited (logically) by the nature of what he has made',[26] must not that logical self-limitation include also the possibility of direct divine intervention? The account of God's relation to his creation that I have been developing does not seem to have room for such a notion, for reasons that are as much religious as philosophical.

If we were to abandon the concept of miracle as a distinct form of direct divine causation, would that imply a wholly negative attitude towards the tradition of miracle in Christian history? Or could there be a revised way of understanding it, parallel to that which I have been suggesting in the case of prophecy, whereby the religious significance of the tradition could be preserved or even enhanced? Certainly miracle has always been seen as more than wonder. The religious meaning of the acclaimed miracle has been regarded as more important than the bare fact of direct divine causation; where no religious meaning can be apprehended we speak not of miracle but of coincidence. The accounts of the gospel miracles themselves, especially in the Johannine record, lay more stress on their spiritual significance than on the outward happening. And this emphasis is strongly developed in early Christian teaching. Origen, for all his allegorizing, did not doubt the factuality of Jesus' miracles; but he insists that the conversion and spiritual transformation of human lives are 'greater works than the physical miracles which Jesus did' – the 'greater works' that Jesus promised to his disciples (John 14.12).[27] So there is nothing untraditional in Mary Hesse's claim that 'for the scientific mind, the miracle stories would not lose their religious depth or effectiveness by such a reinterpretation – rather the reverse'.[28] But even if more important, may not the spiritual meaning be dependent on the miracle literally understood? Religious response, we may allow, is not infrequently set in motion by some event of remarkable or unexpected character. A traveller lost in the desert and rescued in the nick of time by the unlikely and unforeseen arrival of some other traveller may come to see the rest of his or her life as lived on borrowed time. Such a response may be genuinely transformative for good of a person's life, whether that person sees the rescue as fortuitous or as strictly 'providential' – whether indeed it was in fact fortuitous or strictly 'providential'. And what I have described in terms of an individual's experience may also be true of more public events that shape the self-consciousness or destiny of a nation. The Exodus story has frequently been interpreted in just such a way. A fortunate escape from Egypt, combined with the impressive phenomena of Mount Sinai, is seen from the outset as God's great act of deliverance and evokes a lasting and profound commitment of the people of Israel to Yahweh. Literary analysis supports the contention that the more strictly 'miraculous' elements in the story of the crossing of the Red Sea are secondary elements in the development of the tradition. They are the result rather than the cause of its being seen as an act of God.[29] Such a rationalizing account of an ancient saga is dangerously speculative. It is safer to say that the nature of the original happening that first gave rise to such a tradition is lost to us, except in terms of the most tentative reconstruction. But to say that is already to say that much in the miracle tradition has always functioned, and could continue to function, in a way that does not depend on the reality of miracle as a form of direct divine action.

Two questions remain. First, even if it be accepted that there are no compelling reasons for the Christian believer to affirm any form of direct divine intervention in the natural order (indeed that there are good reasons for his or her not doing so), what are we to say of the spiritual concomitants of the miracle tradition, which, it is being suggested, are not merely preserved but even enhanced in their significance? What of the conversions and spiritual transformations of human life that are said to be greater works than the miracles of Jesus? Are they not to be seen as particular acts of God? In the programmatic analysis of Galilee and Hebblethwaite that I have been following, it is claimed that 'the clearest example' of what we are looking for 'is the experience of grace, where a man's conversion, forgiveness, inspiration or enlightenment must be represented as an act of God'.[30] That question I shall be taking up in the next chapter. The second question concerns the person of Christ. Even if the radically revised account that I have offered of God's providential guidance of the world might be acceptable in relation to the history that led up to the coming of Christ, will such an approach, if carried through consistently, allow us to say what Christians need to say about Christ himself? To that question I shall turn in chapter 7.

6

Providence and Personal Life

'To deny providence,' wrote H. H. Farmer, 'is to deny religion.'[1] In the last chapter I outlined what seem to me to be some of the serious difficulties implicit in the idea of God's providential guidance of human history. Within the biblical tradition that is the dominant form in which the idea of providence is to be found. Yet no account of history can fail to concern itself with the decisions and actions of individual men and women. However large the role ascribed to wider political, economic or sociological forces, the decisions and actions of individuals contribute to the particular path that history takes. The actions of a Cyrus or a Judas are more than epiphenomena. Without their actions, the restoration of Israel and the crucifixion of Jesus would either not have taken place at all or would have happened very differently. Moreover the intended goal of the historical process in Christian understanding is also one that concerns itself with individual men and women. The New Covenant foreseen by Jeremiah was still to be made with the people of Israel, but it was to be one in which each person would know the Lord for him or herself (Jer. 31.33–34). Much later Western thought may have erred in the direction of an excessive individualism, but no adequate account of providence can ignore the question of its application to personal life as well as to the public domain of human history. Its need to do so finds powerful symbolic expression in the declaration of Jesus to his disciples that 'the very hairs of your head are all numbered' (Matt. 10.30).

It was precisely providence of this kind that Farmer had in mind when he said that 'to deny providence *is* to deny religion'. For he elaborates that claim by insisting that it is 'undoubtedly true if by providence is meant, not a quasi-philosophical affirmation of an ultimate harmony in things, but a confidence that man's personal life is the concern of a wisdom and power higher than his own'.[2] Many of the issues raised by such a claim are the same as those that we considered in the last chapter when we reviewed the broader application of the notion of providence. I suggested then that there are serious difficulties in envisaging particular divine actions as operative in the natural order or in that comparatively restricted range of human decisions which directly affect the destiny of nations. If we should find ourselves constrained to envisage such particular divine actions as working to further not only the direction of human history as a whole but also the appropriate ends of countless individuals, those difficulties would be greatly increased. But we cannot simply leave the matter there. We need to consider whether any new issues are raised by the application of the idea of providence to individual lives. Moreover if we are led to a reconsideration of the traditional idea of providence in the personal sphere, as I suggested we need to be in the public sphere, is there the same possibility in this second case of a religiously constructive reinterpretation of the older concept? Or is it the case, as Farmer claims, that 'faith in providence and the awareness of God as personal are indissolubly involved in one another'[3] in such a way that no such constructive interpretation is open to us in this case?

How universal is this personal providence of which we are speaking? Is every personal life to be understood to be the concern of a wisdom and power higher than its own? God sends his rain on the just and the unjust alike (Matt. 5.45), but it is the hairs of the disciples' heads that are numbered. No one, that is to say, is excluded from God's wider providence, but it is in the lives of Christians that the special providential care of God is most commonly claimed to be at work. Nothing, therefore, can be more central to the idea of providence and personal life than the way in which a person comes to Christian faith. It is by focussing on that issue that I want to pursue this aspect of our enquiry. 'Conversion' was, after all, the first of those marks of grace in the lives of the saints to which Galilee and Hebble-thwaite drew our attention in the passage which I quoted in the last chapter.[4]

But we must begin a stage further back. Vast numbers die in infancy – old enough to have established themselves as persons in relationships of love with their parents, too young to have established any pattern of personal fulfilment in their own lives. The numbers may be less in the more affluent Western world than they once were. But smaller numbers do nothing to reduce the poignancy of each occasion. And, as we well know, there are parts of the world where the numbers are as vast or vaster than ever. Has the concept of a personal providence anything to say in relation to such happenings? Christians from the early days of the church have attempted to meet the problem in terms of a personal providence. But their attempts to do so are doomed to failure. Gregory of Nyssa devoted a treatise directly to this question, in the course of which he offers this explanation:

> To prevent one who overindulges himself at a party from staying too long at the well-stocked table, he is removed very early from the company of the banqueters; this ensures that he does not succumb to those things to which uncontrolled indulgence gives rise in a glutton. That is how a perfect providence achieves its ends; it not only heals present evils but forestalls them before they arise. And that, I suggest, is the cause of the deaths of new-born infants. He who does nothing without a reason is out of his love for the individual, withdrawing the material for evil; it is a matter of one, whose character is well-known to God through his foreknowledge, being allowed no time to display his true nature by the actual commission of wicked deeds when his propensity to evil would have had the opportunity to show itself.[5]

It is difficult to know whether the purported love to the individual or the eternal foreknowledge of future vice is the more open to objection. However we come to terms with this aspect of our experience (and I tried to outline the sort of way in which it seems to me we have to do so in chapter 4), it cannot surely be in terms of particular providential acts of God. But early Christian thought did not rule out the possibility that even those who died in infancy might in their short lives achieve the most important goal for any man or woman – the coming to a saving relationship with God. The issue was one particularly discussed by Augustine. For him baptism was essential to salvation. In the case of infants, who had no sins of their own to be laid to their account, what was vital was that they should receive baptism for the remission of the penalty of original sin. And so it would seem that contingent factors concerning the availability or otherwise of baptism must be what would determine the eternal salvation or loss of the child. But for Augustine it was God who has to be seen as the true determinant of the issue of human salvation. So the providential guidance of God must be controlling both the availability of baptism and whether or not it was in fact administered. 'Often,' he writes, 'when the parents are eager and the ministers prepared to give baptism to infants, still it is not given, because God does not will it to be given and so does not keep the child alive for the short time needed.'[6]

There is no need to argue against such a position, because it would be difficult today to find any upholder not only of its conclusion but even of the underlying assumptions in terms of which the argument is couched. Yet the basic issue remains. Why does one person become a Christian and another not? As with the baptism of an infant, external factors of upbringing and opportunity clearly play a significant part. But they do not constitute the whole story, even at the human level. There is also the human act of faith. How is that human act of faith related to the choice and call of God? At one stage Augustine proposed that God's call of one person and not another (Jacob, for example, and not Esau – Rom. 9.13) was based on foreknowledge of the faith of the one and the unbelief of the other. We have already considered some of the difficulties implicit in such a form of divine foreknowledge, but they need not concern us at this point, for Augustine himself abandoned the idea – though for a very different reason. It still left the crucial determination of who does and who does not become a disciple in human hands; it detracted unacceptably from the sheer gratuity of divine grace. In the end, therefore, Augustine felt himself forced to accept the logic of his position. The distinction had nothing to do with any difference between Jacob and Esau – present or future. It was a difference in the call of God. 'Many are called but few are chosen' (Matt. 22.14). So God may call both, but it is a difference in the nature of the calls that accounts for why one call elicits the response of faith and the other does not. Not many have followed Augustine all the way down that predestinarian road. But Christians have been much less ready to go back on the religious convictions that drove him along it. Thus Gerald Bonner describes Augustine's teaching about predestination and reprobation as 'only a more rigorous expression of what the Christian must hold, if he is not to fall into Universalism – a theology which has never been acceptable to the mind of the Church'.[8]

Our present interest in the question of conversion is focussed on the claim that it provides unmistakable evidence of particular acts of God. Any account of it that involved the kind of divine control described in the later works of Augustine is clearly incompatible with the general account I have given of God's relation to the world. Is there any other way of understanding God's call, the particular action of God indicated by the experience of conversion, which will be acceptable both to our general account of God's relation to the world and also to the mind of the church, without incurring Bonner's implicit criticism of achieving that acceptability by lack of rigour, by offering in effect a more confused and woolly-minded version of the Augustinian view?

There is no doubting the religious desire to ascribe the glory for one's own conversion to God. After all, to acknowledge the radical dependence of our lives on a gracious reality other than ourselves is an integral part of what it is to come to faith in God.

It is a common enough experience also at the human level for the recipient of love or friendship to insist that all the credit (if the word is appropriate in that context at all) for the joy and benefits of that love and friendship should be ascribed to the generosity of the other rather than to him or herself. The neutral observer may understand why people put it in those terms, but is likely to insist that their words must not be taken too literally. It takes two to make a friendship as well as to make a quarrel. However generous or outgoing the lover or friend may be, there is need also for readiness on the part of the other to accept what is offered. Augustine himself, before the harder stance of his later years, makes just this point:

> It is God who brings about in a man even the will to believe, and in all things his mercy goes before us; yet to consent to the calling of God or to refuse it belongs to our own will. So far from conflicting with the text, 'What hast thou which thou hast not received?', this actually confirms it. For the soul cannot receive and possess the gifts referred to there, except by consenting. What it is to possess, what it is to receive, pertains to God: but the receiving and the possessing necessarily pertain to the one who receives and possesses.[9]

To ascribe to God not only our call but our response as well would, he implies, involve not so much an error in judgment as an error in conception. It would be to make an affirmation that has no meaning. As a matter of logic, only the recipient can be the subject of an act of receiving. The same point is well made by John Lucas. He insists that a Christian, believing as he must in human freedom, 'cannot refuse to speak in the first person. I did it: I could have done otherwise, but I chose to do it.' But having said that and meant it, the Christian then

> attributes all to the grace of God rather than himself, meaning by the grace of God all those factors which he recognizes as having been at work in his own conversion . . . apart from himself. Grace is thus a negative

concept. It is the noun corresponding to the 'Yet not I' of the Christian disavowal of credit.[10]

The value of using the personal analogy of love or friendship is that it can help to free us from a false conceptuality in which divine grace and human freedom are seen as competing explanations, so that the more one ascribes to the former, the less can be ascribed to the latter. That is not how genuinely personal or social interaction works. What is not so clear is whether it necessarily points, as Galilee and Hebblethwaite suggest, to the affirmation of a particular divine action. Of course, the occasion is particular by definition. It is my conversion, at a particular moment in human history and in my life, of which we are speaking. Many factors, not of my doing, have come together and impinged upon me at that moment, and it is these that I acknowledge as the 'Not I' of my conversion and ascribe with gratitude to the grace of God. But these may take many forms, such as the gradual pressure of circumstance, the sudden challenge of an unexpected moment of personal crisis, or the attractive presentation of the gospel by friend or preacher. And happenings of this sort, our earlier analysis has suggested, may better be seen as characteristic aspects of a world that in its totality constitutes God's action rather than as particular or discrete acts of God. In some cases, it is true, a crucial feature of the story may be apprehended as a more direct form of divine address – to a Saul on the Damascus Road or an Augustine in the garden. Cases of that kind seem to offer the clearest examples of where particular divine actions might be located. But before we go on to consider how we should best interpret them, I want first to look again at the more general issue with the help of a rather different analysis.

It is a special concern of process theology, as we saw in chapter 2, to provide an account of divine agency which will also do justice to human freedom and human responsibility. In relation to the operation of divine grace Cobb and Griffin insist, as I have been doing, that one 'cannot divide up responsibility for an action, supposing that the more God is responsible for

what occurs, the less human beings are responsible, or the more
human beings are responsible the less God has to do with it'.[11]
They aim to avoid this misconception by stressing that God
always works by way of persuasion and not coercion. God
contributes to every human action by way of offering to it the best
possibility for the future. Two difficulties attend such an
account. What is meant here by 'offering'? When Cobb says that
God 'confronts believers and unbelievers alike with the ideal
possibility for self-actualization', does this mean more than that
such an ideal possibility always exists?[12] David Pailin clearly
implies that it does. He speaks of God setting before each entity
the range of possibilities open to it and 'highlighting' the one
ideal possibility.[13] But it is not clear in what such 'highlighting'
consists. In the case of human beings it can hardly be claimed that
it involves bringing to awareness what the ideal possibility is in
every case. Yet without something like that the so-called divine
action seems nothing more than a description of the conditions
under which all human action takes place. But even if that
difficulty could be overcome, such an account of God's grace at
work remains a universal truth; it is the way in which God is
always and everywhere at work in the world. If God is always
offering the best possibility for the future, there seems little room
for particular acts of grace. The difference in the outcome of
different occasions would seem to be due to human freedom, and
to lie in part at least with the varied experience with which
different human agents come to each occasion. But John Cobb is
not content to see God's activity only in this universal way. He
uses the human analogy that, without resorting to coercion, we
can direct our hopes and intentions with particular strength
upon particular people. So, he argues,

> it would be arbitrary to deny to God this freedom to
> differentiate his relations to particular occasions. Hence, we
> may suppose that God may well take the initiative in
> presenting himself to human occasions with peculiar force and
> specific efficacy prior to and quite independently of their self-
> preparation or desire for this occurrence.[14]

Moreover, the stress of many religious traditions on the futility of human effort towards salvation leads Cobb to believe that this is not only possible but is in fact the case.

The general question with which we are concerned in this chapter is the question of how we should understand the idea of a divine providence in relation to the life of each individual person. And we have been pursuing the issue in terms of the more particular question: Why is it that some people come to faith and some do not? The most we can claim so far is to have clarified some of the constituent elements that must have a place in any answer that might be put forward. In the first place the mystery of a genuinely free human choice must not be eliminated.

> Two people may have the gospel preached to them in the same way, and have the same opportunities of hearing God's call for each, and one may hearken and the other harden his heart. We ask 'Why?'. No answer can be given except that the one decided to and the other decided not to.[15]

If the Christian experience is 'I; yet not I, but the grace of God', the initial I is not simply cancelled out by what follows. A variety of external factors will also have had an important role to play. But if we were right to doubt the appropriateness of ascribing such external circumstances to the particular direction of God's providence in the wider historical case, it seems even less appropriate, as John Lucas says, to suggest in relation to each individual personal life that God has ' "fixed" external circumstances in order to set the stage for us to play out our life-drama on'.[16]

If that is right, then what remains for us to consider is the possibility of locating particular divine initiatives in the call of this or that individual with 'peculiar force or specific efficacy' on particular occasions. What sense can be given to such a special divine call? It would not remove the mystery of the free human choice, for the divine initiative that we are postulating is of a persuasive and not a coercive nature. It is not therefore open to precisely the same objection as Augustine's unacceptable account of God's elective call of Jacob and his non-elective call of Esau. It is not a question of some divine calls being accompanied and some unaccompanied by the divine choice. Human freedom is preserved. Yet it is not wholly free from objections of essentially the same kind. If we speak of God's call having 'peculiar force or specific efficacy' in some cases, that logically implies a lesser degree of force and efficacy in others. The apparent arbitrariness in a divine will that operates in such a way remains, and remains a serious objection to accepting such a picture.

Our use of the analogy of human personal relationships was designed to overcome the sense of conflict between divine grace and human freedom. It has proved helpful in that respect. But it has still left us with a serious problem. For it is precisely this same personal analogy that strengthens our desire to speak of particular divine initiatives. Not to do so would be, in Cobb's view, an arbitrary denial in God's case of a freedom enjoyed by human beings. It is not perhaps surprising to meet with such an argument in a process theologian, since it is a basic feature of process theology that it qualifies the absoluteness of God's transcendence and sees him as one actual entity among others. But it is precisely this aspect of process theology that I have criticized in an earlier chapter.[17] And it is not only process theologians who argue in this way. The argument is equally common in theologians with a more traditional approach to God's transcendence. I quoted some very similar words from David Brown in the last chapter: 'If man has such a freedom, it would be rather surprising if God did not possess the same kind of freedom to act without causal restraint in the world.'[18] The argument is both clear and impressive. Personal initiatives of this kind are integral to our lives as human persons. Not to assert such initiatives in the case of God would seem to make him, the ground and source of our existence as persons, less fully personal than we are. But the argument is not without its difficulties. Personal language in relation to God is a form of analogy (albeit the primary analogy for speaking about God) and not direct description. God is not a person as we are. There are important aspects of our existence as embodied persons, our sexuality for example, which we do not ascribe to God. So too there are aspects of our existence as finite persons, the gradual acquisition of knowledge through the senses for example, which we do not ascribe to God. More significantly it has been my argument throughout that God's creation of our world necessarily implies a divine self-limitation in relation to traditional understandings of omnipotence and omniscience. May it not be that the same principle of divine self-limitation is operative at this point also? If so, it would not be a matter of God lacking the fundamental personal characteristic of initiating action that we enjoy. For the ongoing creation of the world is God's free act. If Solomon chooses to entrust the building of the temple wholly into the hands of his stonemason, he logically cannot take any further particular initiative in the matter without going back on his original free decision, though that fact involves no diminution of his interest in the enterprise or of the very important sense in which it is his act. So to deny to God the 'freedom to act without causal restraint in the world' may not in fact be to depersonalize him but be rather a corollary of the kind of world God has in fact chosen to create.

But even if it be granted that the view I am putting forward does not amount to a depersonalization of God in himself (since I am continuing to speak of God's free personal act in the creation of the world as a whole), it still has another serious objection to overcome. Whatever may be true about its implication for God in himself, does it not depersonalize our relation with God? And does it not thereby undermine the deepest convictions and values of Christian faith? In other words, if we do away with the traditional understanding of particular divine acts of providential care and guidance in our lives, can we offer any alternative and religiously acceptable account of those aspects of Christian faith which have found expression in such forms of thinking and believing?

A full (or, to put the point more modestly and certainly more appropriately, a fuller) answer to that question must await the final chapter, when I shall try to relate the understanding of

God's action that I have been giving to Christian practice as a whole, and to Christian prayer in particular. But my basic claim (as in the case of providence and history) is that the account that this approach enables us to offer, so far from weakening, actually strengthens a properly personal form of faith. Accounts of conversions and what has led up to them are necessarily retrospective in character. They are examples of the fundamental human process of the search for meaning. Two things are particularly characteristic of such a search. We find meaning by giving a unified narrative account of our lives and by relating their individual meanings to the larger meaning of God's purpose for the world as a whole. So Paul, the passionate missionary to the Gentiles, sees that meaning as determinative of his whole life and envisages God not merely calling him on the Damascus road but setting him apart for that task from his birth (Gal. 1.15). So Augustine, called back in his middle years from the life of contemplation to public office as Bishop of Hippo, seeks through the writing of *The Confessions* to understand his calling in terms of God's dealings with him from the first moments of his life.[19] In all such cases a story is told in terms of God's active preparation, call and guidance of the person's life. Understand that language of divine action too literally and the rich personal purpose which the language was designed to illuminate is undermined or diminished. For read such stories forwards instead of retrospectively and there is no escape from the arbitrary election, implausible disposition of external circumstance and unacceptable manipulation of inner life. Why then the language of God's action at all? Because our lives are a part of God's personal act in the bringing into existence of the world, a world which includes as a paramount part of its purpose the self-dedication of human lives such as those of a Paul or an Augustine. It is precisely in them that God's act finds part of its fulfilment, not because there are separate distinguishable divine initiatives in relation to them or to particular aspects of them but because the emergence of such lives is what God's one act deliberately seeks to make possible.

7

God's Action in Christ

One of the many difficulties in the study of christology is the variety of issues involved – biblical exegesis, history of doctrine, philosophical problems. Even a full length treatment of the subject hardly provides the scope, and few scholars have the competence, to deal adequately with all these basic constituents of the question. To treat of it, therefore, in a single chapter in this book is to run the risk – perhaps indeed to ensure in advance succumbing to the risk – of superficiality. Yet to deal with christology as a distinct subject among others within theology and to devote a whole book or a whole course of lectures exclusively to it has its own dangers. For whatever form our christology may take, it can hardly exclude the affirmation that for the Christian the life of Christ is the supreme example of God's action in the world. Yet with so many other items on the agenda, many discussions of christology treat the idea of God's action as if it were a comparatively straightforward concept and regard the heart of the problem as how to expound the special character of that action in the case of Christ. But what I have said so far has shown, I hope, even if it has achieved nothing else, that the idea of divine action is itself a highly problematic concept, that cannot be clarified without careful consideration of a wide range of issues, such as creation, evil, providence, grace and freedom. And this broader issue of God's action in the world has not received the degree of attention it deserves as a directly theological problem. To remedy that lack is the central concern of this book. So in what I have to say about Christ, I do not propose to take up – let alone, pretend to solve – all the varied problems involved in the study of christology. My aim is the more limited one of exploring the two-way interaction that there needs to be between the questions of how we are to understand the figure of Christ and how we are to understand God's action in the world.

In the last two chapters I brought under review the traditional understanding of both historical and personal providence. The New Testament presentation of Jesus sees him unhesitatingly in terms of providence of both kinds. He is the climax of a long historical process. He is born in the fullness of time (Gal. 4.4), and brings to fulfilment things that had been pointing forward to him in every part of scripture (Luke 24.44). Furthermore all that happens to him as an individual follows a similar providential pattern. The early moves of his opponents against him were ineffective 'because his hour was not yet come' (John 7.30; 8.20); and everything that did happen, including his final arrest and death, was in accordance with 'the determinate counsel and foreknowledge of God' (Acts 2.22–23). Such language raises no new or special problem. The issues are not different from the ones I considered in those earlier chapters just because they are applied to Jesus. I suggested then that such language is best understood as a form of retrospective interpretation of experience. Approached in that way in the case of Jesus, the language that I have quoted will be understood as the early Christians' way of making cosmic and personal sense of the life of Jesus and its significance for the world and for them. It can, I believe, be accommodated without too much difficulty into the revised, retrospective view of providence that I have been proposing.

But with the central doctrines of the incarnation and resurrection of Christ it is a different story. If the difficulties that I have been raising about particular divine actions and about miracle are valid, it is not easy to see how these central affirmations can be exempted from their challenge. Yet that is what many Christians, seeking to do justice both to critical and to traditional insights, are inclined to do at the present time. And it is not hard to see why. 'The incarnation is,' in John Macquarrie's phrase, 'the supreme providential act or miracle of history.'[1] And that supremacy has normally been understood to imply not merely that the person of Christ and the events of his life are of central importance for the life of faith but that they are distinct in kind. It has never been easy to spell out precisely the nature of that distinctness. It is tempting, therefore, to see in the reinterpretation of other claimants to be cases of divine intervention or miracle along the lines that I have been suggesting an opportunity for clarifying the distinctness of the incarnation and the resurrection. May not they be seen as unique cases of special divine action, of a kind which in the past has mistakenly been claimed to be the pattern of God's acting on a much wider scale? But such a view has awkward implications which are vividly expressed by Leslie Houlden in a review of a recent book on divine revelation, when he writes:

> The isolation of incarnation and resurrection as prime and crucial instances of direct divine action, while it may seem a concession to modernity, effectively falsifies the role they formerly played. Once peaks in a landscape full of hills, all seen as such instances, they now stand out like naked pillars of rock in a plain.[2]

It distances Jesus from the rest of history in the kind of way that led Marcion to see him as the emissary of some higher God, other than the creator.

For reasons of this sort, theological as opposed to popular reaction to the idea of treating incarnation and resurrection as such radical exceptions to the normal pattern of God's dealing with the world has been generally unfavourable. And this negative reaction is shared by critics and upholders of the traditional doctrines alike. It is perhaps not surprising to find Michael Goulder speaking of 'the implausibility of a theology which allows that the world has been going for four billion years and posits only two actions of God, one 1982 and one 1952 years ago'.[3] But David Brown reacts in a very similar way, if with a diametrically opposed solution to the problem raised. 'Unless,' he writes,

> one is prepared to endorse an interventionist view of God (that over and above his general ordering of the world there are certain specific actions which he performs within our historical, temporal framework), then the very idea of an Incarnation will inevitably seem such a startling exception to the uniform pattern of God's relation to the world as to be, quite literally, incredible.[4]

It is worth noting that his opposition to any understanding of the incarnation as 'a unique exception to the normal pattern of divine activity' is not based simply on its incredibility. He declares a little later on that his principal reason for rejecting such a view is a religious one, namely that it would mean that 'Christ's experience would have no analogy to our own and thus be of no clear relevance to us'.[5]

So the case against treating incarnation and resurrection as divine acts of an altogether unique kind seems to me a very strong one. David Brown's acceptance of that case leads to a strengthening of his conviction that a wholeheartedly interventionist account of God is what we ought to adopt generally. The wide range of theological considerations, which have formed the main substance of this book so far, hold me back from taking that route. The alternative road that I propose to follow is, therefore, to ask whether there are ways in which the convictions traditionally embodied in the doctrines of incarnation and resurrection can be preserved by the opposite move of seeking to bring them within the pattern of understanding God's action that we have developed so far.

The two doctrines are not on all fours with one another. Brian Hebblethwaite shares David Brown's conviction about the validity and necessity of traditional incarnational doctrine, but is strongly opposed to any idea of divine intervention. He regards it as 'not unreasonable to suppose that even the Incarnation is achieved without breaking the structures of the natural world', but he goes on to describe the resurrection as 'a different kettle of fish'.[6] We need therefore to deal with them separately.

The basic witness of the New Testament writers is to the decisive nature of God's action in and through Jesus. The God who had spoken in fragmentary and varied fashion through the prophets had spoken a final word through his Son (Heb. 1.1–2); in Christ God had been reconciling the world to himself (II Cor. 5.18). Later christological doctrine is the reflective judgment of the church as to what must be true about the person of Jesus, if that conviction is valid. The classical form of the resultant doctrine was the two-nature christology formally affirmed at the Council of Chalcedon. Its ascription of a full human nature to Christ, against the general tendency of some influential earlier theology and against the explicit affirmation of some of the more attractive forms of Christian heresy, is significant. It rules out certain ways of understanding the specialness of God's action. It was not through a person whose constitution was so unique that his humanity was apparent rather than real. It was not, of course, intended to exclude the miraculous as an important aspect of God's action in Christ. After all Christians believed that God could and did do miracles through the agency of ordinary men and women. Moreover the miracles of Jesus were sufficiently distinctive in their eyes for Leo's *Tome* (which was officially endorsed by the Council of Chalcedon at the same time as the promulgation of the two-nature christology) to speak of the divine nature of Christ as the agent of his miracles while the human nature was the recipient of his sufferings, albeit each nature acting in conjunction with the other.[7] But that way of speaking has generally been regarded as highly unsatisfactory and too divisive of the unity of Christ. The divine and the human do not act separately. However precisely God's action in Christ is to be understood, it is in and through a full human nature. In the later language of primary and secondary causation, God's special action towards the world in Christ is not a matter of the suspension of secondary causation. The special-ness of the divine act is not achieved by eliminating the human. The action of God in Christ comes through the acts of the human Jesus.

If that was the thrust of the early church's considered teaching, maintained against the main swim of both the intellectual and the devotional tide, it is even more definitely the emphasis of most contemporary christological writing. The full humanity of Jesus is widely seen as involving the recognition that he, like every other human person, was a product of the evolutionary process, one whose particular characteristics were substantially affected by his heredity and environment with all the attendant limitations of psychology and knowledge. It implies also ascribing to him that same genuine freedom which is constitutive of our existence as human persons. Affirmations of that kind are to be found in the writings of many who seek to maintain a highly traditional understanding of the incarnation as well as of people who advocate some substantial revision of it.[8]

What account of God's action in Christ can be given that will be congruent with such an understanding of him as a human person? Many of those who have had the courage to attempt some answer to that question have very sensibly taken as their starting-point the experience of God's action in the lives of other men and women, God's prophets and God's saints. From there they have gone on to attempt some extension of their understanding of the interaction of God's grace and human freedom in such cases which might do justice to the specialness of God's action in Christ. Many excellent books on christology have been written along these lines. But one problem seems always to remain. Is the perfection of human response, that in the case of Jesus is claimed to go along with God's grace towards him, a full and adequate description of what we intend in speaking of the incarnation? If it is, then the incarnation raises no new problem for our analysis of God's action in the world; it will simply constitute a particular case within whatever is the appropriate understanding of God's grace in human life more generally.

But many Christians feel that such an approach does not do justice to the special nature of God's action in Christ. Three attitudes may be distinguished. Some, like Professor Lampe in his Bampton lectures, would claim that it is all that can be properly said without undermining the authentic humanity of Jesus, while acknowledging that it is not identical with what the early church thought itself able to affirm in terms of the hypostatic union.[9] Others, while pursuing their reflections along the same lines, argue that it must ultimately lead to a conclusion fully in line with the traditional dogmatic teaching. Thus Donald Baillie claims that the attempt to understand the person of Christ in terms of the 'paradox of grace' gives rise in the end to the confession 'that while the life lived by Jesus was wholly human, that which was incarnate in Him was of the essence of God, the very Son of the Father, very God of very God'.[10] Although he comes out of a very different philosophical and confessional background, the heart of Karl Rahner's christology is very similar. In what is offered as an elucidation of the meaning of the hypostatic union, he says that Jesus 'is a man who just like us receives in his spiritual, human and finite subjectivity the self-communication of God in grace which we assert of all men'; the distinction, as the continuation of the sentence quoted puts it, is that the case of Jesus is 'the climax of development in which the world comes to itself absolutely and comes to the immediacy of God absolutely'.[11] But in both these cases, critics have objected that for all the orthodoxy of their language and of their intentions, the accounts that they give fall short of what incarnational doctrine is designed to affirm. So we may distinguish a third group, who, while, not wishing to repudiate the descriptive account of God's action in Christ that we have given, want to insist very strongly that beyond that and as its ground we need to assert the life of Jesus 'quite literally to *be* the human life and death of God himself in one of the modes of his own eternal being'.[12]

The differences between these three attitudes are not absolute, as the difficulty of assessing the christologies of Donald Baillie and Karl Rahner bears witness. But it is not germane to our purpose here to decide between them. For despite the radical differences in their accounts of who Jesus is, none of them speaks of any different kind of *action* of God in relation to the world. It was after all Brian Hebblethwaite, whom I have here taken as representative of the strongest affirmation of incarnation, whom I quoted earlier in support of the view that the idea of incarnation did not involve any breaking of the structures of the natural world. Whether or not we finally decide that there are good reasons for speaking of the life of Jesus as also 'the life . . . of God himself in one of the modes of his own eternal being', it would seem that as long as we are determined to continue affirming the genuine humanity of Jesus, there is no difference in kind as far as God's action in the world is concerned between the case of Jesus and the case of other human persons. In both cases the sense in which the actions done are God's actions, the sense in which they may be said to embody particular divine initiatives, has to be compatible with the sense in which they are also full and free human actions. How that leads us to speak about Jesus and his actions will therefore be intimately related to what we say about the operation of God's grace elsewhere.

We cannot develop that in detail now. But it is perhaps worth giving one example of its implications, if we accept the account of God's grace that I developed in the last chapter. There I gave special attention to the question of election and God's call. I suggested that talk of God's call of Paul before his birth was not to be understood literally as implying some particular act of ante-natal preparation or even foreknowledge on the part of God. It was rather a retrospective way of affirming how completely the service of God through mission to the Gentiles had been deter-minative of Paul's active life. In the case of Jesus, then, it would be appropriate to understand in a similar way talk of his pre-existence or of his being sent into the world or of the Spirit's overshadowing agency in the arrangement of his birth. These would be seen, not as particular divine acts ensuring the birth of the particular person, Jesus, but rather as a retrospective way of expressing the totality of his commitment to and fulfilment of the will of God for the world.

But my present purpose is simply to claim that it seems possible – indeed, one may even say necessary – to incorporate any acceptable interpretation of the special action of God in Jesus within the overall account I have been giving of God's more general action in providence and grace. But what of the resurrection? Is that, in Brian Hebblethwaite's uncharacteristically colloquial phrase, 'another kettle of fish'? Certainly he is not the only one to think so. Anthony Hanson, in his book *Grace and Truth*, gives a thoughtful exposition of the incarnation as God's supreme revelation in the completely human which, he insists, does not involve any acknowledgment of miracle or of the superhuman as a necessary element within it – with one exception. And that is the resurrection, which in his view is essential to that revelation and has to be acknowledged as a superhuman event.[13] There are many who would agree with him. But if he is right in what he claims, the whole line of argument that I have been developing would be undermined. Michael Goulder's two special actions in the whole of human history might be reduced to one. But one action of so distinctively different a kind would be sufficient to call in question the claim that the absence of divine intervention in relation to so many evils and disasters in the world is because such direct action is logically incompatible with the kind of world that God has chosen to create. Is there then any way of understanding the resurrection which does not have such drastic implications?

Certainly there are theologians who believe that such an understanding is possible. Hans Küng, in his widely read work, *On Being a Christian*, asserts roundly that 'the raising of Jesus is not a miracle violating the laws of nature . . . not a supernatural intervention which can be located and dated in space and time'.[14] But if it is not, how is it to be understood? The question needs to be tackled both historically and theologically. What those two approaches lead us to say may not be identical, but they must be consistent. Here, as in the case of the incarnation, the problems are complex and I shall not begin to address the full range of issues. I shall be restricting myself to one question: is there a way of understanding the resurrection of Jesus, consistent with the more general account of God's relation with the world that I have been outlining, which can also meet the proper demands of responsible historical and theological reflection?

I begin with the empty tomb and the physical aspect of the resurrection, of which the empty tomb is certainly the symbol though not the proof. Most scholars are agreed that within the development of the tradition, it is the appearances that are primary and the empty tomb that is secondary. But to be a secondary feature of a tradition does not necessarily involve being a false or untrustworthy element within it. On that issue scholarly opinion is clearly divided. My own judgment, not surprising in the face of such a division of opinion, is that the evidence is indecisive. Historically the issue has to be left wide open. Theological reflection begins with the universally agreed insistence that in speaking of the resurrection of Jesus, we are speaking of something more than the resuscitation of a corpse; we are speaking of a transformation to a new kind of life, not of a return to human existence as we know it. Nevertheless, though a physical resurrection is certainly not to be seen as the whole story, it may be (and usually has been) claimed to be an essential element within the whole. But it is not easy to see why it should be regarded as theologically necessary. Whatever Christians may properly mean by their hope for the resurrection of the body, it cannot reasonably be understood to involve continuity of our existing bodily substance. And in view of that fact, it is hard to see how such bodily continuity could be a theological necessity in the case of Jesus' resurrection. That argument is not only used by Hans Küng to support his non-miraculous understanding of resurrection, but has also helped to convince a much more conservative scholar like David Brown that the 'Empty Tomb is not even a necessary condition for the truth of the Resurrection' since the survival of death is not related to what happens to the body of the person who has died.[15]

But even if there is no need historically or theologically to affirm any special divine intervention in relation to the body of Jesus, that by itself does not amount to showing that it is possible to provide an adequate account of the resurrection which does not involve any special divine action or intervention. We have acknowledged that the primary form of the resurrection tradition is that which speaks of the appearances of Jesus. Moreover those appearances are presented as the cause rather than the product of the emerging Christian church and its distinctive resurrection faith. Historically the tradition is a strong one and it is not easy to give an alternative account of the emergence of the church and of its faith. But historical reflection by itself cannot determine the nature of such appearances or visions. A wider range of considerations has to be brought into play before we can judge whether we ought to envisage them as special acts of God.

When we turn to the theological tradition, we meet with a similar picture. There too the resurrection is seen as the basis not the product of faith. But care needs to be exercised in interpreting that epigrammatic claim. Before the resurrection there already existed firm faith in God, a God who in the conviction of many could raise the dead; and some had already responded to Jesus as the decisive proclaimer of God's kingdom. The resurrection is to be seen, perhaps, not so much as the basis but rather as the coping-stone of a distinctively Christian conformation of belief. It seems to me no clearer theologically than historically that this final coping-stone, faith in the vindication of Jesus and the conviction that Jesus lives in the presence of God, could only have derived from some special action of God in the form of supernaturally given appearances of Jesus.

In his big book, *Jesus*, Schillebeeckx attempts a detailed account of how such faith might validly have arisen without ascribing a unique and supernatural character to the 'appearances' of Jesus. His account has many difficulties, as he would be the first to admit. 'As to the way in which the divine source of that assurance took a historical form,' he writes, 'discussion on exegetical grounds could be endless.'[16] But equally serious difficulties attend more traditional accounts, when they are prepared to spell themselves out in similar detail. David Brown is right when he suggests that what for him 'is sufficient to tip the balance towards endorsement of the objectivity of the disciples' experience' will appear 'highly doubtful unless one has *already* accepted a theistic, as distinct from a deistic, interpretation of God's activity in the world'.[17] But it is precisely his interventionist account (he explicitly identifies 'theistic' with 'interventionist' and 'deistic' with 'non-interventionist'[18]) that I have been arguing throughout this book is both implausible and full of difficulty for a reasoned Christian faith. So for me the balance tips the other way. I do not wish to underestimate the difficulties in my own position, either when it comes to giving a historical account of what followed the death of Jesus or to giving a theological justification of my faith in God as supremely revealed in Christ. But I do not believe that the difficulties in either of those spheres are as great as the difficulties that would arise were I to bring into those accounts the category of some distinctively different form of divine action.

In conclusion it is worth recalling what I have and what I have not been attempting to do in this chapter. It has not been my aim to expound or to defend a particular doctrine either of the incarnation or of the resurrection. I approached my task with a rough sketch of how we might most appropriately understand the idea of God's action in the world already in mind. That picture had been built up from wide-ranging experience of life and of traditional Christian teaching about creation, providence and grace. I had argued in earlier chapters that we can make best sense of this whole complex of experience and of ideas if we think of the whole continuing creation of the world as God's one act, an act in which he allows radical freedom to his human creation. The nature of such a creation, I have suggested, is incompatible with the assertion of further particular divinely initiated acts within the developing history of the world. God's act, like many human acts, is complex. I have argued that particular parts of it can rightly be spoken of as specially significant aspects of the divine activity, but not as specific, identifiable acts of God. That way of looking at it, I have hinted (though this has yet to be more fully developed in the final chapter), not only makes for a more intelligible but in the long

run also for a more religious account. But one obvious objection
has been hanging over the whole enterprise. However attractive
on other grounds, does not the Christian understanding of
Jesus and of his resurrection simply rule it out *ab initio*? My aim
in this chapter has been to meet that objection. I have not, of
course, attempted to do so by making the absurd claim that
incarnation and resurrection have never been intended or
understood in ways which would have that effect. But our
understanding of incarnation and resurrection cannot in any
event be unchanging, any more than can our understanding of
any other aspect of Christian doctrine. What I have tried to
argue is that there are ways of understanding both doctrines
that are consistent with my more general account of God's
action in the world and which, however revisionary, do not
simply deny their central concerns, but may even help some of
those concerns to find more adequate expression. That – and no
more than that – is what I have tried to do. But if the case is
sound, it would be an important contribution to the perennial
search for a reasoned and vital faith.

8

God's Action in Us

I began this book by posing a dilemma that is deeply felt by many reflective Christians – on the one hand the difficulty of giving any convincing account of how God acts in the world and on the other the conviction that a 'God who no longer plays an active role in the world is . . . a dead God'.[1] Can Christian faith escape succumbing to either implausibility or death? I may, I suspect, appear to have done more to restore plausibility than life. But no religious person can accept that a dilemma posed in those terms represents a real choice. Truth and life belong together. If my approach to the understanding of God's action in the world is along the right lines, it cannot be destructive of true faith. So from time to time in the discussion of particular aspects of our problem, I have attempted to suggest how the view that I have been proposing might contribute positively to the life of faith. In this final chapter I want to consider more directly the implications of my position for the life of prayer and worship, as a distinctive and central aspect of Christian life.

In a sensitive and probing article about petitionary prayer, Helen Oppenheimer raises the kind of problem with which I have been concerned. 'Is there,' she asks, 'any room in the universe for the kind of "particular providence" which real answers to petitionary prayer would have to be?'[2] Her fundamental approach to the problem is summed up in these terms:

> The required assumption is that in some fashion God does act
> in the world. What petitionary prayer involves is that,
> granted this, human beings may become associated with the
> divine activity.[3]

She emphasizes the 'in some fashion'. How God acts in the
world is 'the aspect of the problem,' she says, 'that has to
remain "pending".'[4] I do not want to claim that my discussion
removes it from the pending tray. But my aim has been to
explore as well as I am able in what fashion God acts in the
world. The strategy I propose to follow in this chapter is,
therefore, first to sum up the understanding of how God acts to
which I have come, and then to go on to ask, as Lady
Oppenheimer proposes we should, how human beings may in
prayer become associated with a divine activity so understood.

I have argued that there is one act (in the sense of a piece of
intentional behaviour initiated by an agent) that we may and
must affirm to be God's act, namely the continuing creation of
the universe. The complexity of this 'act' does not invalidate its
being described as a single act. At the human level we regularly
apply such a description to complex happenings, such as the
building of Solomon's temple. A complex action of that kind
necessarily contains within itself a number of secondary
actions, which together help to make up the one complex act.
Gordon Kaufman, to whose treatment of this topic I am much
indebted, speaks of the process as a whole as God's 'master-act',
and then goes on to speak of 'subacts performed by God as he
works out his purpose'.[5] The illustration that he uses of the
relation between a subact and the complex act of which it is
constitutive (namely, a carpenter hammering nails and a
carpenter nailing boards together to construct a house) suggests
a need to speak in such terms.[6] But, as I have argued earlier, a
master-act may be made up of subacts whose agent or agents are
other than the agent of the master-act. Solomon's building of
the temple necessarily involves many subacts, but he does not
himself have to be the agent of any of them in a sense
distinguishable from his being agent of the one master-act. And

in the account that I have given of divine activity I have not
followed Kaufman in speaking of God performing any of the
subacts which together contribute to God's one act of creating
our world.[7] I distinguished four types of happening or action
which have traditionally been seen as the main forms of God's
action in the world, but in each case (though for varied reasons)
the description of them as acts (or subacts) performed by God
seemed to me inappropriate or at least in need of some very
careful and highly qualified interpretation. It will be helpful to
list the four and characterize their differing relationships to the
one master-act of God as creator of the whole.

1. There are the regular patterns according to which the
physical world operates and which are known to us (in so far as
they are known) through the study of the natural sciences.
These regularities have allowed for the emergence of life and
increasingly complex organisms. Their amazing potential for
giving rise to human life and human consciousness derives from
the fact that they owe their existence to God's one act of
creation. In that sense they are by their very nature an
expression of the divine activity. But I have argued that their
very regularity militates against the appropriateness of speaking of them, even in the significant stages of the emergence of
new forms of life, as acts of God in any further or distinguishable sense (Chapter 3).

2. There are some happenings where the normal patterns of
observed behaviour do not appear to operate and some of these
are spoken of as miracles. If we were to speak in terms of 'laws of
nature', we would have to say that those laws of nature were
broken in such cases. If we prefer to speak rather of statistically
determined regularities of observed behaviour, it would not be
enough in the case of those happenings designated 'miracles' to
speak of them as exceptional cases which might at some later date
be brought within the framework of some revised scientific
account. The claim in those cases is that their occurrence is due to
some specific action of God designed to further God's purpose in
a particular situation. I have argued that there are insufficient
grounds for claiming that such cases exist (Chapter 5).

3. There are actions by human agents, who have no conscious intention to further any believed purpose of God, but which do in fact achieve results that Christians believe to be of great significance for the furtherance of that divine purpose. Those actions may or may not at the same time be successful in achieving the quite different (and sometimes evil) intention of the human agent. I have argued that, however great the coincidence of the result of such an action and the furtherance of God's purpose in the world, it is inappropriate to speak of it as an action of God. There does not seem to be any intelligible way of relating the intention of God and the human deed performed, which would be a necessary condition for describing it as a specific action of God. When St John puts into the mouth of Caiaphas the words 'it is expedient that one man die for the people' and goes on to comment that 'he did not say this of his own accord' (John 11.50–51), we should not take the words at their surface level and puzzle over how the divine puppeteer prompts the high priest to speak such prophetic words. It is rather a matter of the dramatic irony of the evangelist vividly portraying the important truth that the evil intentions of men and women do on occasion bear fruit that will be for the healing of the nations (Chapter 5).

4. There are actions by human agents, who freely intend to further the purposes of God, seek God's grace to enable them to do so, and do in fact achieve their intended goal. Here the relationship to God's act is much closer. But even in such cases the problems concerning divine grace and human freedom make it uncertain whether and in what sense one can appropriately speak of them as God's acts (Chapter 6).

Since actions of this last type are not only those most intimately related to the activity of God but are also those most immediately involved in the life of prayer and worship which is our present concern, we must consider in rather more detail how they are most appropriately to be understood in relation to the action of God. The way in which we speak about action at the human level varies in accordance with the purpose and style of our speaking. All significant human actions have a complex ancestry. For certain purposes it may be sufficient and true to say 'I chose to do it and there's no more to be said'. But for other purposes (for example, if I want to contrast my action with that of someone from a very different cultural background) I may go on to talk about a wide range of social expectations and social restraints. I may even make the point by saying it was my upbringing that led me to act as I did. Nor need there be any conflict between those two accounts, if I have so internalized that upbringing that it works with and not against the grain of my choosing. Nor indeed is the use of language, including action language, always intended to be understood in a directly descriptive way. Human speech fulfils many roles and the appropriate style of speech varies accordingly. 'It's all thanks to you! It's all your doing!', I may say to the friend who has stood by me and encouraged me to make my own choice. That is a proper use of language in the context of the expression of gratitude, though it would be misleading if taken literally as a straightforward account of the genesis of my action. Since so much religious language has its place in a context of thanksgiving, the analogy may not be without significance.

With these examples in mind, let us turn to a consideration of Christian prayer and worship. And we shall do so with two expectations. First, we ought to expect that problems about the relation of such prayer to God's action may well remain incapable of solution as long as we approach them in terms of the particular occasion of prayer alone, without giving serious attention to the 'complex ancestry' of that occasion.[8] Secondly, we ought to expect to find considerable divergence in the use of language about God's action in the very different contexts of worship and of critical reflection. Such differences may well appear to amount to direct contradictions at the surface level, without actually involving real contradiction when appropriately understood from within their different contexts.

Despite the gospel promise, 'Whatever you pray for in faith you will receive' (Matt. 21.22), it has always been recognized that there are some things which it is absurd to pray for because they conflict with the given structures and regularities of the world. Thus Origen could write:

> It would be utterly absurd for a man who was troubled by the scorching sun at the summer solstice to imagine that by his prayer the sun could be shifted back to its spring-time place among the heavenly bodies.[9]

Once that principle is acknowledged, it is difficult to define its limits. I have argued against the reasonableness of expecting any special divine modification of the physical ordering of the world. I do not therefore propose to discuss prayers of that kind, but rather prayers for God's grace. To do so does not rescue us at a stroke from the kind of difficulty I have been adumbrating. Does not such a move, it can be objected, however popular in today's church, involve essentially the same kind of divine intervention as the prayer for change in the external world? The objection is raised by unbeliever and believer alike. Thus Michael Goulder argues that the deflection of an Exocet missile and the deflection of Mrs Thatcher's judgment would involve equally crude forms of divine intervention – with the implication that both forms of praying had better be abandoned.[10] Stuart Hall argues very similarly that to stop 'praying against bad weather, drought, flood, storm and pestilence' and to pray instead for the generosity needed to respond to such adversities 'does not in fact get rid of the difficulties it perceives' and is both 'illogical and seriously atheistic' – but with the apparent implication in his case that we should go back to the older forms of praying.[11] Both support their case by arguing that psychological change itself involves a form of physical change in the brain circuits. But their conclusion does not follow from the fact that psychological changes may always involve concomitant changes in the brain circuits; their argument would only be valid if we were to hold a false form of physical determinism according to which psychological change could only be brought about by a prior modification of the brain circuits. Nevertheless the substantive point they make is not without force. My own misgivings about any direct ascription of election or conversion to some special action of God were of a similar character.[12] Can prayers for the grace of enlightenment or for the grace of spiritual strength be understood in ways that are free from such objections?

Certainly the most immediately obvious interpretations of such forms of prayer do seem to run into difficulties of this kind. Praying to God for enlightenment may suggest that we are looking for a way to understanding that bypasses the normal critical procedures; praying to God for strength may suggest that we are looking for a way to achievement that makes the customary expenditure of effort unnecessary. But however much the outcome of our praying may seem to confirm such expectations, that kind of interpretation is to be firmly rejected. It is neither necessary nor desirable. Insight in any field of understanding may come at unexpected times and in unexpected ways. To ascribe such knowledge to a direct divine source, with the implication that it is therefore exempt from critical scrutiny, is to open the floodgates to fanaticism. The person who prays for strength may learn that his previous efforts were a hindrance to achievement. But he might have learnt the same lesson to relax and not strive too hard in a non-religious context; what is involved may be more properly seen not as the replacement of human activity by divine, but rather as the substitution of a more appropriate form of human acting. Again we may picture our prayers as giving rise to knowledge not otherwise accessible to us or as providing strength beyond the limits of our normal psychological capacity. Such pictures spring naturally enough out of the obvious human analogies. A friend enlightens us on issues that fall within the competence of his or her experience but lie outside our own; or he adds his strength to ours and enables us to achieve some feat that we could not have done single-handed. But here too the concept of a special divine communication of an additional quantum of knowledge or strength above that which would have been accessible to us naturally is highly unsatisfactory. The picture follows too closely the analogy of one human person's relation with another. And even at the human level, as soon as we move beyond the more trivial examples and seek to understand the full range of mutual enlightenment and co-operation between individuals within human society, we are aware of a need to extend the scope of our reflections before an adequate answer can be given. We are faced, as we foresaw, with the need to take into account what I have called the more 'complex ancestry' of our prayers for grace.

What then is the nature of this broader account? Prayers to God have their place within a continuing story, and just because they are prayers to *God* they cannot be adequately understood in isolation from that full story, however immediate or precise the language in which they are expressed. That story is the story of God's action in the creation of the world. The mysterious phenomenon of human consciousness has arisen in it not by chance, but as a result of the intention that constitutes the world God's act. The capacity to attain, however incompletely, some awareness of that intention is a part of what it is to have been created free beings in God's image. Such recognition, and very partial realization, of God's purpose as the world has seen in the past have been primarily forwarded by those who have used their God-given potential to open themselves to and identify their own goals with what they have grasped of the will of God. In the language of process theology they have responded to the lure of the divine love available to them, and it is that that has enabled them to contribute to this still very partial recognition and realization of God's will. And we, in our turn, stand on their shoulders. Apart from them we would be in no position to be seeking God's grace in prayer in the way that we do.

This dependence on the ways in which God's intention has found its very partial fulfilment so far is not evenly spaced in relation to past history nor does it simply take the form of reaching back and learning from that past. For the Christian the figure of Jesus as presented in the New Testament stands out. He stands out as a fulfilment of many early intimations of God's purpose for the world, as in himself the fullest expression of that divine intention for human life and thereby as creative of future possibilities of appropriate response to God. But the transformative power of Jesus is not something that exists only in the past, available to us as we go back in search of it. It has transformed the world by giving birth to new images and symbols, which in making possible new ways of perceiving the world thereby make possible new ways of living in it. These new ways of perceiving the world find expression not only in the belief systems of the church, but also in the imaginative creations of poets and artists and in the varied forms of Christian worship. Particularly important examples are the sacraments of baptism and eucharist, which in this perspective are more clearly seen as effective, and not merely commemorative, symbols of Christ's death and resurrection. In other words the divine intention does not only find expression spasmodically in the lives of the saints occurring at scattered points in human history; it also finds more institutional expression (though still, of course, very incomplete expression) in a Christian vision of the world, particularly as enshrined in the sacraments of the church.

This then is the fashion of God's acting in the world – making possible the emergence, both individually and corporately, of a genuinely free human recognition and response to what is God's intention in the creation of the world. And it is with this that we associate ourselves in prayer and worship. Indeed our association of ourselves with it is not merely a means towards its furtherance in other aspects of life (though it is that), but is also itself a part of the fulfilment of that purpose.

Little objection will, I think, be raised against such an account of the 'complex ancestry' in the light of which our individual acts of prayer and worship are to be understood. But is it a sufficient account? I have stressed a number of strands that constitute the indispensable background conditions of any particular experience of grace: God as the ultimate source of the conditions in which our lives are set; the availability of an awareness of his purpose of love as a source of guidance for our lives; the ways in which that love, having been apprehended and responded to in the past, is accessible to us now in such forms as the writings of the saints and the sacraments of the church. And just as there is a cumulative response to God in human history embodied in the continuing life of the church, so there is a cumulative response in individual human lives. We do not come to particular occasions of prayer for God's grace as newly minted or unformed entities. We come with characters developed in specific ways, ways partly determined by the extent to which we have opened ourselves to God's grace in the past. But even when all that has been said and full allowance has been made for its contribution to the form and effectiveness of our prayers for grace, the question remains: does not our account need to be completed by an insistence on some supervenient personal address of God, involving the kind of particular divine action postulated by Galilee and Hebblethwaite?[13] Whatever the difficulties such a concept may pose for the understanding, it may seem that unless we allow for some such specific address within our account, we will be unable to give a religiously satisfying description of prayer. The most we would be doing, it might appear, would be to give a description of prayer as a means of bringing our lives into relation not so much to God as to some generalized conception of God's will for the world.

That difficulty, though widely felt, can, I believe, be dissolved by more careful reflection and analysis. The nature of God's action in creating a world of which genuinely free human creativity is a vital constituent can only be spoken of in the most general of terms. For God's purpose is no pre-packaged blueprint to which men and women must conform or be broken. Our human actions affect the way the world develops for good and ill. It is God's will that they should. So God's will for the world can properly be spoken of not only in the generalized form that characterizes his one fundamental act of creation; it can also be spoken of in more precise and changing ways that take account of how the world now is as a result both of human achievements and of human sin. But what that more particular will of God is at any time is something we have to discover; it is not directly given and we need to exercise great caution in any claim to know what it is. And what is true about the world at large is true about our individual lives also. We are not born into the world with a predestined role to fulfil – or to frustrate and be frustrated. When we speak of God's will for our lives as individuals at a particular time, as we may, it is always an open concept of which we are speaking. Since human freedom is an integral part of God's purpose in the creation of the world, his will for individual human lives must also be one that allows us freedom to choose between various ways in which our potentialities may be developed and used; it is something that is always open to change in the light of past choices and actions both our own and others'. This open and creative character of the search to discern and to realize God's will for our lives serves to make the whole process a profoundly personal one. Our prayers for grace are an integral part of that search. In them we are not involved merely in an intellectual attempt to discover what God's will for us might be; we are involved in bringing to special awareness the fact of the presence to us of the God whose will we are seeking. And that presence, like the presence of the human friend which prompts us to say 'It was all thanks to you! It was all your doing!', needs no particular identifiable initiative to give it its significance.[14] So what seems at first to be a depersonalizing interpretation, because it leaves no place for a specific divine initiative, turns out in the end to have precisely the opposite effect. It not only avoids the age-old difficulties inherent in ideas of election – why this person is called and not that, why this prayer is answered and not that; it can also claim to offer a more deeply personal and thereby a more deeply religious account of grace as a whole.

If that is an adequate account of the way in which our prayers for grace are related to the activity of God, why should prayer take the form that it does? In our prayers we ask God to do things in a way which certainly suggests particular individual divine actions in response to our requests. The language we use is, of course, very largely language that we have inherited, and it has been understood in very different ways at different times and in different places. But even allowing that it is open to a variety of interpretations, is it compatible with the kind of account that I have been giving? In any response to that question, it is vital to begin by recalling the different styles of language appropriate to religion and to theology. The language of religion, like the language of poetry, uses the direct and concrete image to make vivid for us the underlying realities of our life. That is the only way in which they can be brought to bear imaginatively and effectively upon the well-springs of our being. But it is easy to be misled in the process of spelling out what such imaginative language involves. Indeed the task on which I have been involved throughout the course of this book has been an attempt to counteract some misconceptions that arise when such religious language is understood too simplistic-ally. And my goal in so doing is not to wean us away from the use of such language altogether (though we may well be led to want to modify it in some respects), but rather to enable us to use it in a way which does not conflict with other aspects of our understanding of life.

It may seem to some that what I have actually done is to replace a simplistic view of religious language with a highly sophisticated, or even sophistical one. Yet a little reflection will show, I believe, that I have only been extending more widely and consistently an approach that is in fact shared even by the most conservative believer. Christians have always prayed and continue to pray with the utmost regularity 'Give us this day our daily bread'. How is such a prayer to be interpreted? It has the particularity not merely of direct request to God, but of a request to be met today. Yet we are not asking God for a supply of manna that would increase the unemployment rate among bakers. Nor are we asking God to influence the mind of the secretary of the Bakers, Food and Allied Workers' Union against the option of calling for a strike. What we are doing, surely, is acknowledging the givenness of the world, with its remarkable physical balance which has made possible the emergence of human life and the conditions to sustain it. But with that acknowledgment goes also the recognition that it is human creativity that has learnt and is still in process of learning how best to use those conditions for the growing of the corn and that it is co-operative human labour that is needed to turn it into bread. Moreover the inclusive 'us' reminds us that if the prayer is to be fulfilled for Ethiopian children, as well as those in the Western world, there will have to be a development of managerial skills and a radical reordering of priorities that are a challenge both to our creativity and to our values. It expresses in concrete form the same fundamental petition as the clauses that stand alongside it in the Lord's Prayer, for the doing of God's will and the coming of his kingdom. So it is not a straightforward petition. It appears to be asking for God to do something quite specific now, but that is not how we understand it. Nor do we regard ourselves as behaving in an unreasonably sophisticated, let alone sophistical, manner when we refuse to take it in that way. The broader interpretation I have suggested is as natural to us as the directness of its linguistic form is welcome and appropriate.

If that is an acceptable analysis of this central clause of the Lord's Prayer, why are we so hesitant to allow a similar analysis in other cases? Other forms of prayer to God to do things and other affirmations of what God has done or is doing are patient of the same basic kind of interpretation. And many of the problems that arise through critical reflection invite such an approach. It may sound sophisticated, or even reductionist, at first in contexts where we are not used to its application. But it is not really so. We ought not to wait until we are forced to make a series of such moves separately in relation to each particular form of petitionary or intercessory prayer or in relation to each specific example of purported divine action, as one by one more traditional interpretations become too implausible to maintain. We should rather be seeking to develop over a broad field the kind of understanding of divine action that I have been seeking to commend as a constructive and religiously helpful style of interpretation.

How can that understanding be best set out in summary form? God's fundamental act, the intentional fruit of the divine initiative, is the bringing into existence of the world. That is a continuous process, and every part of it is therefore in the broadest sense an expression of divine activity. Differences within that process, leading us to regard some happenings as more properly to be spoken of in such terms than others, are dependent not on differing divine initiatives but on differing degrees of human responsiveness. The players in the improvised drama of the world's creation, through whom the agency of the author finds truest expression, are not ones to whom he has given some special information or advice, but those who have best grasped his intention and developed it.[15] The personal character of God's love is shown in the fact that the world that he is bringing into being is designed to elicit a fullness of personal life through the exercise of freedom. The additional affirmation of particular divine acts in the form of special immediate or mediated divine initiatives seems at first hearing to enhance that basic Christian conviction about the personal character of God. What the survey of the areas of Christian teaching that we have considered in suggests is that that teaching does not need to be understood in a way which requires us to make that further claim, and that if we do so it does not in fact strengthen a personalist account of Christian faith in the way we would initially expect. Moreover, although the idea cannot be simply ruled out as logically impossible, the difficulties of integrating it into an awareness of the world that seeks to take full account of recent developments in human knowledge are enormous. A modified account of divine agency along the lines that I have been suggesting here is not without its own problems. But they do not seem to me as severe as those that other accounts have to face.

'The God who no longer plays an active role in the world is . . . a dead God.'[16] Walter Kasper's phrase, 'playing an active role in the world', may not be an appropriate description of the God whose agency I have been seeking to describe. But that God is no dead God. He is the living God, the source of all life and the source of that authentic life which his worshippers seek to realize in grateful awareness of his all-pervasive and sustaining presence.

NOTES

1. Where Does God Act?

1. See J. Hick and M. D. Goulder, *Why believe in God?*, SCM Press 1983, p. 81.
2. *The Times*, 10 July 1984.
3. *The Times*, 20 June 1985.
4. *The Guardian*, 31 July 1984. The leading evangelical critic of the Bishop of Durham, David Holloway, remains unconvinced by the Archbishop, and claims that his own opposing view would have had the support of William Temple. See D. Holloway, *The Church of England: Where is it going?*, Kingsway Publications 1985, p. 213.
5. W. Kasper, *The God of Jesus Christ*, SCM Press 1984, p. 24.
6. G. E. Wright, *God Who Acts*, SCM Press 1952.
7. B. Albrektson, *History and the Gods*, Lund 1967, cited by J. Barr, 'Story and History in Biblical Theology', in *Explorations in Theology* 7, SCM Press 1980, p. 13.
8. Frank Dilley, 'Does the "God who acts" really act?', *The Anglican Theological Review* 47, 1985, pp. 66–80. This article, together with the two mentioned in the next two notes and others on the same topic, is also to be found in a useful collection of articles on this subject in O. C. Thomas (ed.), *God's Activity in the World* (AAR Studies in Religion No. 31), Scholars Press 1983.
9. By S. M. Ogden in *The Reality of God and Other Essays*, SCM Press 1967, pp. 164–187.
10. By G. D. Kaufman, *Harvard Theological Review* 61, 1968, pp. 175–201. Also in G. D. Kaufman, *God the Problem*, Harvard University Press 1972, pp. 119–147.
11. The phrase 'distantly analogous' is used by Austin Farrer in *Faith and Speculation*, A. & C. Black 1967, p. 23, with specific reference to divine causality.

2. God the Creator

1. Justin Maryr, *1 Apology*, 59.
2. Tertullian, *Adversus Hermogenem*, 21.

3. Origen, *De Princ.*, 2.1.5; *Com. Jn.*, 1.18. (The two texts are II Maccabees 7.28 and Shepherd of Hermas, *Mandates*, 1.1.)

4. J. Cobb and D. Griffin, *Process Theology*, Westminster Press 1976, p. 65.

5. Cf. the comment of P. Hefner: 'The chief clue to [Griffin's] grasp of the problem of evil is the . . . enormously significant rejection of the traditional *creatio ex nihilo* doctrine.' ('Is theodicy a question of power?', *Journal of Religion* 59, Jan. 1979, p. 90.)

6. J. Cobb, *A Christian Natural Theology*, Lutterworth Press 1966, p. 143.

7. The language is that of H. H. Farmer. See his *Towards Belief in God*, SCM Press 1942, p. 52.

8. Cobb and Griffin, op. cit., p.65.

9. Calvin, *Institutes of the Christian Religion* I, xvi. 1.

10. Ibid., I, xvi. 3.

11. Ibid., I, xvi. 8.

12. Ibid., I, xvi. 4.

13. Ibid., II, iv. 2.

14. Thomas Aquinas, *Summa Theologiae* 1a, 19, 8.

15. Ibid., 1a, 22, 4.

16. Ibid., 1a, 23, 3.

17. A. N. Whitehead, *Process and Reality*, Macmillan 1929, pp. 11 and 135 (corrected edition, D. R. Griffin and D. W. Sherburne, Free Press 1978, pp. 7 and 88).

18. J. Cobb, op. cit., p. 211.

19. David A. Pailin, 'God as Creator in a Whiteheadian Understanding', in H. Holz, and E. Wolf-Gazo (eds), *Whitehead and the Idea of Process*, Verlag Karl Alben 1984, p. 285. On the concept of 'necessity' in relation to God's creative activity, see. p. 27, below.

20. K. Barth, *Church Dogmatics* II/1, T. & T. Clark 1957, p. 587.

21. Thomas F. Tracy, *God, Action, and Embodiment*, Eerdmans 1984, pp. 143–4.

22. Grace M. Jantzen, *God's World, God's Body*, Darton, Longman & Todd 1984, p. 152.

23. S. Kierkegaard, *Christian Discourses* (tr. W. Lowrie), Oxford University Press 1959, p. 132.

24. C. Hartshorne, 'The God of Religion and the God of Philosophy' in G. Vesey (ed.), *Talk of God*, Macmillan 1969, p. 158.

25. See Thomas Aquinas, *Summa Theologial*, 1a, 13, 7; 1a, 45, 3.

3. The Creation and God's Action

1. Aquinas, *Summa Theologiae*, 1a, 19. 2.

2. Ex. 33.11; Ex. 20.21.

3. J. McMurray, *Self as Agent*, Faber & Faber 1969, p. 204. The title of that final chapter is 'The World as One Action'.

4. Ibid., p. 220 (italics original).

5. G. D. Kaufman, 'On the meaning of "Act of God"' in *God the Problem*, Harvard University Press 1972, p. 137 (italics original).

6. M. Goulder and J. Hick, *Why Believe in God?*, SCM Press 1983, p. 73.

7. R. Bultmann, *Theology of the New Testament*, Vol. I, SCM Press 1952, pp. 228–9.

8. A. N. Whitehead, *Process and Reality*, Macmillan 1929, p. 69 (corrected edition by D. R. Griffin and D. W. Sherburne, Free Press 1970, p. 43). Griffin and Sherburne note the suggestion that 'decision' may be a mistake for 'decisions'. I owe this reference to D. A. Pailin, 'God as Creator in a Whiteheadian Understanding' in H. Holz and E. Wolf-Gazo (eds), *Whitehead and The Idea of Process*, Verlag Karl Alber 1984, p. 296.

9. J. V. Taylor, *The Go-Between God*, SCM Press 1972, p. 31.

10. A. M. Farrer, 'The Prior Actuality of God' in *Reflective Faith*, SPCK 1972, p. 191.

11. Farrer, *Faith and Speculation*, A. & C. Black 1967, p. 82.

12. Farrer, *Saving Belief*, Hodder & Stoughton 1964, p. 52.

13. Farrer, *A Science of God?*, Geoffrey Bles 1966, pp. 87–8.

14. Ibid., p. 104.

15. Hugh Montefiore, *The Probability of God*, SCM Press 1985, p. 161.

16. Theodore of Mopsuestia was forced into the desperate expedient of claiming that Paul intends us to contrast man's relation to God with that of the clay to the potter. A man, unlike the clay, *can* answer back! (See K. Staab, *Pauluskommentare aus der Griechischen Kirche*, Münster 1933, pp. 145–7.) Modern commentators are more inclined to say with C. H. Dodd that at this point Paul's 'thought declines from its highest level', *The Epistle of Paul to the Romans*, Hodder & Stoughton 1932, p. 158.

17. Farrer, *A Science of God?*, pp. 76–7.

18. D. Sayers, *The Mind of the Maker*, Methuen 1941, p. 23.

19. Ibid., p. 54.

4. Whence Comes Evil?

1. See P. Brown, *Augustine of Hippo*, Faber & Faber 1967, p. 46. 'Only this group [the Manichees], Augustine thought, could answer the question that had begun to "torment" him as soon as his "conversion" to philosophy had caused him to think seriously: "From what cause do we do evil?" The Manichaean answer to the problem of evil is the core of the Manichaeism of the young Augustine.'

2. See G. D. O'Brien, 'Prolegomena to a Dissolution to the Problem of Suffering', *Harvard Theological Review*, 57, 1964, pp. 301–23.

3. P. Hefner, 'Is Theodicy a Question of Power?', *Journal of Religion* 59, Jan. 1979, p. 89.

4. Paul Ricoeur, 'Religion, Atheism and Faith' in *The Conflict of Interpretations*, Northwestern University Press 1974, p. 455.

5. Ibid., p. 461.

6. Ibid., p. 460.

7. C. Hartshorne, 'The God of Religion and the God of Philosophy' in G. Vesey (ed.), *Talk of God*, Macmillan 1969, p. 159. Cf. also C. Hartshorne, *A Natural Theology for Our Time*, Open Court, La Salle 1967, pp. 116–21, esp. p. 117: 'Job's mistake was in supposing he knew what is meant by unsurpassable or divine power.'

8. Cf. Basil Mitchell's parable of the Stranger in A. Flew and A. Macintyre (eds), *New Essays in Philosophical Theology*, SCM Press 1955, pp. 103–5.

9. See Augustine, *Opus Imperfectum contra Julianum*, 5, 1.

10. G. Bull, *Works ii Discourse V*, pp. 125ff. (cited by N. P. Williams, *The Idea of the Fall and Original Sin*, Longmans 1927, pp. 361–2).

11. See Augustine, *De Libero Arbitrio*, 2, xx, 54.

12. Theodore of Mopsuestia, *Commentary on Galatians* 4, 24 in H. B. Swete (ed.), *Minor Epistles of St. Paul*, Cambridge University Press 1880–2, 1, 74–5.

13. P. Tillich, *Systematic Theology Vol. II*, Nisbet 1957, p. 50.

14. P. Ricoeur, *Symbolism of Evil*, Beacon Press 1969, pp. 251–2.

15. See Cobb and Griffin, *Process Theology*, p. 69.

16. This is the nub of J. L. Mackie's careful argument against theism from the problem of evil in *The Miracle of Theism*, OUP 1982, pp. 164–76. His discussion is directed against a theism which envisages a stronger sense of divine control than is argued for here. Nor does it consider the issue of moral *growth* and personal *development*.

17. See C. Butler, *An Approach to Christianity*, Collins 1981, p. 134.

18. L. Gilkey, 'Providence in Contemporary Theology', *Journal of Religion* 43, July 1963, p. 175.

19. See p. 29 above.

20. See pp. 24–5 above.

21. The phrase is taken from J. A. T. Robinson, *In the End, God*, James Clarke 1950, p. 123. Dr Robinson told me that his source of the citation was N. Berdyaev, *The Destiny of Man*, Geoffrey Bles 1937, p. 273, where the phrase is again ascribed to Origen without specific reference. I believe it to be Berdyaev's epigrammatic summary of Origen's view rather than an exact citation.

22. See M. F. Wiles, 'The Resurrection of the Body' in *The Remaking of Christian Doctrine*, SCM Press 1974, pp. 125–146.

23. F. Dostoevesky, *The Brothers Karamazov*, Heinemann 1948, Book 5, ch. 4, p. 252.

5. Providence and Public History

1. J. Macquarrie, *Principles of Christian Theology*, revised edition, SCM Press 1977, p. 239.

2. See p. 44, above.

3. J. Macquarrie, op. cit., p. 246. Peter Geach uses the same analogy to argue for a much more particularized understanding of providence than Macquarrie envisages. ' "On that square", says the Grand Master, "I will promote my pawn to Queen and deliver check-mate to my adversary": and it is even so.' P. Geach, *Providence and Evil*, Cambridge University Press 1977, p. 58.

4. J. R. Lucas, *Freedom and Grace*, SPCK 1976, p. 39.

5. See p. 28, above.

6. Charles M. Wood, 'The Events in which God Acts', *Heythrop Journal* XXII, 3, July 1981, pp. 278–84.

7. D. Galilee and B. Hebblethwaite, 'Farrer's Concept of Double Agency: A Reply', *Theology* LXXXV, Jan. 1982, p. 9.

8. See pp. 34–6, above.

9. See p. 3, above.

10. Eusebius, *Demonstratio Evangelica* III, 7, 30–3.

11. Ibid., *Historia Ecclesiastica* VIII, 16, 1–4. The reference is to the Emperor Galerius.

12. A. M. Farrer, *Faith and Speculation*, A. & C. Black 1967, esp. pp. 159 and 66. I have developed my criticisms of Farrer's position in 'Farrer's Concept of Double Agency', *Theology* LXXXIV, July 1981, pp. 243–9.

13. V. Brümmer, *What Are We Doing When We Pray?*, SCM Press 1984, p. 122 n. 12.

14. See J. R. Lucas, op. cit., p. 7.

15. Ibid., p. 31.

16. B. L. Hebblethwaite, 'Predestination and Divine Foreknowledge', *Religious Studies* 15, Dec. 1979, pp. 440–1.

17. See C. H. Dodd, *According to the Scriptures*, Nisbet 1952.

18. Thomas Aquinas, *Summa Theologiae* 1a, 105, 6.

19. F. G. Kirkpatrick, 'Understanding an Act of God' in O. C. Thomas (ed.), *God's Activity in the World*, Scholars Press 1983, p. 178. Cf. D. J. Bartholomew, *God of Chance*, SCM Press 1984, p. 142: 'Although the body/mind relationship is perplexing, each of us has little doubt that what we will in our minds is translated into the movement of our limbs and our pens. Though this may seem incredible, it actually happens. It does not, therefore, seem too far-fetched to suppose that God is able to express his thoughts through matter in some analogous way.'

20. David Brown, *The Divine Trinity*, Duckworth 1985, p. 20.

21. See pp. 79–80, below.

22. Cf. F. Schleiermacher, *The Christian Faith*, T. & T. Clark 1928, p. 183: 'As regards the miraculous, the general interests of science, more particularly of natural science, and the interests of religion seem to meet.' And J. Macquarrie, op. cit., p. 249: 'If miracle in the sense of supernatural intervention is irreconcilable with science and history, it is also objectionable theologically.'

23. J. R. Lucas, op. cit., p. 9. Cf. also p. 31: 'God can always interfere.'

24. Brian Hebblethwaite, *Evil, Suffering and Religion*, Sheldon Press 1976, pp. 92–3. This is a recurring theme in Hebblethwaite's writings. See also 'Providence and Divine Action', *Religious Studies* 14, June 1978, p. 234 (where Hebblethwaite differentiates his position from Kaufman's view that the whole idea of divine causal intervention is inconceivable) and 'Pre-destination and Divine Foreknowledge', *Religious Studies* 15, Dec. 1979, pp. 447–8.

25. See Chapter 4, 'Whence Comes Evil?'.

26. See p. 63, above.

27. Origen, *Contra Celsum*, 2, 48. For this and other examples, see M. F. Wiles, 'Miracles in the Early Church' in C. F. D. Moule (ed.), *Miracles*, Mowbrays 1965, pp. 223–4.

28. M. Hesse, 'Miracles and the Laws of Nature' in C. F. D. Moule (ed.), op. cit., p. 41.

29. See W. G. Pollard, *Chance and Providence*, Faber & Faber 1958, pp. 106–110; Malcolm Diamond, 'Miracles' in *Religious Studies* 9, Sep. 1973, p. 307; J. Macquarrie, op. cit., pp. 250–3; D. Brown, op. cit., p. 66, who goes so

far as to say that 'historical investigation can rule out a miraculous crossing of the Red Sea'.

30. See p. 57, above.

6. Providence and Personal Life

1. H. H. Farmer, *The World and God*, Nisbet 1935, p. 99.

2. Ibid., p. 92.

3. Ibid., p. 93.

4. See p. 57, above.

5. Gregory of Nyssa, *On the Deaths of New-Born Infants* (PG 46, 185c).

6. Augustine, *De Dono Perseverentiae*, 12, 31. See the discussion in E. Te Selle, *Augustine the Theologian*, p. 324, where this passage is cited.

7. See W. S. Babcock, 'Augustine and Paul: the case of Romans IX' in ed. E. A. Livingstone, *Studia Patristica* XVI, Berlin 1985, pp. 473–9.

8. G. Bonner, *St Augustine of Hippo*, SCM Press 1963, p. 389.

9. Augustine, *De Spiritu et Litera*, XXXIV, 60.

10. J. R. Lucas, *Freedom and Grace*, p. 13. It is interesting to compare the opening sentence of Lucas' essay on Providence. 'The concept of providence is a negative concept', op. cit., p. 27.

11. See Cobb and Griffin, *Process Theology*, p. 157.

12. J. B. Cobb, *A Christian Natural Theology*, Lutterworth 1966, p. 232.

13. D. A. Pailin, 'God and Creation – a Process View', *Epworth Review*, Jan. 1982, p. 83. Pailin himself no longer holds the view expressed in the article for the kind of reason given in the text.

14. J. B. Cobb, op. cit., p. 237.

15. J. R. Lucas, op. cit., p. 14.

16. Ibid., p. 34.

17. See pp. 19–20, above.

18. See p. 65, above.

19. Cf. P. Brown, *Augustine of Hippo*, pp. 163–5.

7. God's Action in Christ

1. J. Macquarrie, *Principles of Christian Theology*, revised edition, SCM Press 1977, p. 303.

2. J. L. Houlden, review of W. J. Abraham, *Divine Revelation and the Limits of Historical Criticism* in *Journal of Theological Studies* XXXIV, April 1983, p. 378.

3. J. Hick and M. Goulder, *Why Believe in God?*, SCM Press 1983, p. 87.

4. D. Brown, *The Divine Trinity*, Duckworth 1985, p. x.

5. Ibid., p. 8.

6. B. L. Hebblethwaite, 'Providence and Divine Action' in *Religious Studies* 14, June 1978, p. 235.

7. Leo, *Tome* 4.

8. This fact was brought home to me very clearly in the discussion to which the publication of *The Myth of God Incarnate* gave rise. See my contribution to M. Goulder (ed.), *Incarnation and Myth*, SCM Press 1979, p. 4.

9. See G. W. H. Lampe, *God as Spirit*, OUP 1977, reissued SCM Press 1983, pp. 143–4.

10. D. M. Baillie, *God was in Christ*, Faber & Faber 1948, pp. 150–1.

11. K. Rahner, *Foundations of Christian Faith*, Darton, Longman & Todd 1978, p. 195. Cf. also 'The man Jesus *in* his human reality exists with a created, active and "existentiell" centre of activity vis a vis God and in absolute difference from him. He prays, he is obedient, he comes to be historically, he makes free decisions . . .' (ibid., p. 292).

12. B. L. Hebblethwaite, 'Incarnation as the Essence of Christianity?', *Theology*, March 1977, p. 85. For Hebblethwaite's unqualified insistence on the authentic humanity of Jesus, see his words: 'In no way do we follow the "docetic" tendencies of early Christianity, which found it hard to believe, for example, that Jesus shared the limitations of human psychology and knowledge' (M. Green (ed.), *The Truth of God Incarnate*, Hodder & Stoughton 1977, p. 102).

13. See A. T. Hanson, *Grace and Truth*, SPCK 1975, pp. 20, 63 and 77.

14. H. Küng, *On Being a Christian*, Collins 1977, p. 349.

15. See ibid., p. 351; D. Brown, op. cit., pp. 130–1.

16. E. Schillebeeckx, *Jesus*, Collins 1979, p. 649.

17. D. Brown, op. cit., p. 134 (my italics). Cf. also, for the more general issue, R. Swinburne, *The Concept of Miracle*, Macmillan 1970, pp. 70–1.

18. D. Brown, op. cit., p. x.

8. God's Action in Us

1. See p. 2, above.

2. Helen Oppenheimer, 'Petitionary Prayer', *Theology* LXXIII, Feb. 1970, p. 56.

3. Ibid., p. 63.

4. Ibid., pp. 62–3.

5. G. Kaufman, 'On the Meaning of "Act of God" ' in *God the Problem*, Harvard University Press 1972, p. 143.

6. Ibid., p. 136.

7. See pp. 61 and 80, above.

8. For a fuller treatment of this principle and its significance for theology, see my 'The Holy Spirit in Christian Theology', *Theology* LXVI, June 1963, pp. 233–7 (reprinted in *Explorations in Theology* 4, SCM Press 1979, pp. 67–72).

9. Origen, *On Prayer*, 5, 3.

10. See J. Hick and M. Goulder, *Why Believe in God?*, SCM Press 1983, p. 84.

11. S. G. Hall, 'The Prayer of the Church. What We Ask and How We Ask It', *Expository Times*, Vol. 96, Dec. 1984, p. 76.

12. See p. 81, above.

13. See p. 57, above.

14. This concept of God's presence is more fully developed in my *Faith and the Mystery of God*, SCM Press 1982, pp. 121–4. On its specific application to prayer, see P. R. Baelz, *Does God Answer Prayer?*, Darton, Longman & Todd 1982, p. 50.

15. See pp. 37–8, above.

16. See p. 2, above.

INDEX